Mornings
with
Jesus
Book 2

Mornings
with
Jesus

Seek and you will find...

A 30 Day Journey

Joshua Scott Zeitz

DEDICATION

'Tuck Me In!'

(A dedication from the author to his mother, his Madre,
Jo Annette Lopez)

Several years ago, when I was a child, my mom used to come into our room just before bed to tuck us boys in. There were three of us.

We were adopted.

First, my older brother, then my younger brother and me two years later.

Upon adopting us, it took some time for me to warm up to my mom.

I carried way too much baggage from past trauma into this new family.

But our parents loved us anyhow!

My mom would tell us all about Jesus, about the Bible, about various issues and topics she felt were important.

She did this faithfully each night.

At the time, I didn't appreciate it the way I should have.

Although I did get used to her doing it!

One night in particular, she came into the room like normal, but I had already fallen asleep.

I awoke an hour or so later in a frantic state of confusion!

I hopped off the top bunk and ran into her room.

"You forgot to tuck me! Why didn't you tuck me in?"

I was crying by now and quite hurt thinking that she had forgotten her nightly routine.

She hadn't, however, and she escorted me back to my room and graciously spent some time with me.

You see, up to this point, it was difficult between my mom and me.

I had so much pent-up anger and emotions toward women from my past and much of this caused my trust in her to come quite slowly.

Our biological mom left us and never came back. We were placed in the state's foster care system.

One of the older girls, in the foster care system herself, sexually abused me.

Needless to say, I had a lot of apprehension about women and girls and therefore it took quite some time for me to warm up to my new mom.

I called her by her first name for a while before finally calling her mom.

Years later, during a heavily rebellious stage I walked through, I reverted back to calling her by her name only and even added some other far more derogatory statements!

I was a mess of a person and, sadly, I took out much of my anger on her!

She was so gracious, however, and persistent!

She never backed down and no matter how many times I would push against her, she would continually love on me, telling me about Jesus, about the Bible, and about issues and topics she felt were important.

She was a true woman of God!

I miss the times she used to come in and tuck us boys in.

Recently, this past Thanksgiving, she went home to be with the Lord...

I had the honor of standing by her bedside with many other family members as she took her final breaths.

She opened her eyes wide in her last moments as if she saw something spectacular!

I believe she did.

I believe she saw Jesus!

I like to think that I was able to tuck her in one final time before she drifted off to her eternal rest.

What an awesome woman of God she was! I am very thankful she was so faithful, persistent, loving, and gracious towards me for all those years.

More than 20 years ago, I was radically transformed in a jail cell, and soon afterwards our relationship was restored!

In recent years, I have taken to calling her Madre.

The last time we spoke in person, she met my family and me to pick up some copies of the first devotional I wrote.

She just wanted to show her love and support and give some copies out to some people she knew.

She was always doing that, encouraging me!

The last text message I received from her was her telling me how proud she was of me for sharing the gospel on mission trips.

Even later in life, she never forgot to tuck me in!

Every birthday, every holiday, she was so faithful and gracious!

I love you Madre!

This devotional is dedicated to you.

Thank you for showing me the love of Jesus even when I didn't deserve it.

Thank you for tucking me in!

Your son,

Joshua Scott Zeitz

Jo Annette Apple Lopez
1960 — 2022

Table of Contents:

(Continued…)

Introduction

Welcome to Mornings with Jesus, Book 2, a 30-day Journey! The goal of this devotional is to provide you with a hands-on interactive resource to grow in intimacy with the Lord!

This is the second book of a three-part series. The themes of the three books are **A**sk, **S**eek, and **K**nock: **A.S.K.**

Asking – Learning to come before God with boldness and confidence because of what Jesus has done for us and in us!

Seeking – Delving into the Word of God with gusto, having a deep desire to know God more each day!

Knocking – Persisting in our pursuit of the Lord in spite of our circumstances, feelings, or personal experiences.

Getting to know the Lord more and growing in intimacy with Him is a lifelong pursuit. It doesn't happen overnight.

At the close of each chapter, I have enclosed some challenge questions. Take your time answering these. There is no right or wrong answer. They are meant to help you better know the Lord and to be open and honest with yourself and Him! They are not meant to be followed as an exact formula, but rather to serve as a guide in your journey toward knowing Him more!

Also, at the close of each chapter, I have included a word search using words from that day's devotional. These are meant to help bolster your vocabulary, stimulate your brain, and provide a fun, interactive way to engage in the day's lesson!

Thank you so much for joining me on this journey. My hope is that your Christian walk will flourish as a result!

And if you do not yet know the Lord, my hope is that you will see how much He longs to know you and for you to know Him more!

Thanks so much,

Joshua Scott Zeitz

*"But without faith
it is impossible to please Him,
for he who comes to God
must believe that He is,
and that He is a rewarder
of those who diligently seek Him."*
~Hebrews 11:6 (NKJV)

A.S.K.

"And you will seek Me and find Me, when you search for Me with all your heart." ~Jeremiah 29:13 (NKJV)

Several years ago, my dad, brothers, and I were playing hide and seek out on my grandma's farm. It was getting dark and the places to hide were vast and many.

After the count, we all scattered and went our separate ways. I proceeded to scurry underneath the electric fence and circle back around to where we started. I went inside the house, scooped myself a heaping bowl of ice cream, sat down, and watched television!

Technically, we never said the house was off limits, but I certainly didn't give anyone a fair chance to find me!

Aren't you glad God doesn't do that to us?

Granted, we do have to search for Him, and we do have to scour the Bible at times for real treasures, but He isn't sitting back eating ice cream and laughing at us!

When it comes to seeking in our spiritual lives, this is what I like to call the "oomph factor."

It's one thing to attend church once a week, listen to the pastor rattle off his three points and a scripture, and then go home - forgetting most of everything he talked about.

It's something entirely different to get up in the morning and have the kind of gusto mentioned in the Psalms, *"As the deer pants for the water brooks, So pants my soul for you, O God."* ~Psalm 42:1 (NKJV)

Or what about utilizing something I heard a pastor say, "Bible before breakfast," or emulating the heart and passion of Job, *"I have not departed from the commandment of His lips; I have treasured the words of His mouth More than my necessary food."* ~Job 23:12 (NKJV)

Listen, the devil hides things from us - he is sneaky, conniving, manipulative, and mean, but the Lord hides things for us! He wants us to prosper in every area of life, but sometimes we have to show some oomph if we want to see things come to pass in our lives.

In other words, He's not going to do everything for us!

For example (and I have had to learn this the hard way and am still learning it), God uses people to get things done. But if we isolate ourselves continually from the very people God is trying to use to bless us, how are we going to receive that blessing?

As another example, God likes to set up divine encounters where we can be the answered prayer to someone else's heart cry, but if we are always worrying about ourselves, scurrying through crowds with our heads down, self-consumed, how are we to be the answered prayer? In essence, the Bible says, *"Give and it shall be given..."* ~Luke 6:38 The Lord is trying to provide opportunities for us to give, but when we are too "busy," we miss those chances...

Be encouraged today. God is not a one-stop shop! He has no sign in His store that screams, "You break it, you buy it!"

No, He is full of compassion and He is okay with us failing, falling, and faltering. The key is to never give up, get back up, and seek Him with all your heart!

One last thing for today, here's a quick test to see where your oomph factor lies:

The Bible says, *"A good man out of the good treasure of his heart brings forth good; and an evil man out of the evil treasure of his heart brings forth evil. For out of the abundance of the heart his mouth speaks."*

~Luke 6:45 (NKJV)

Go ahead, give yourself a check-up from the neck up: If the things that are consistently coming out of your mouth are filled with negativity, complaining, doubt, worry, fear, anything that you wouldn't repeat if Jesus or your pastor was in the room, then that's a sure sign that your heart is low on the Word.

Easy fix: Fill up on the Word!

Begin to seek after it with all your heart. Put God first. Seek Him daily, make it a habit!

This is something we ALL struggle with, so don't you dare feel bad, just start right now!

What are you A.S.K.ing the Lord for today? Keep seeking! Don't stop!

"Let us not grow weary or become discouraged in doing good, for at the proper time we will reap, if we do not give in." ~Galatians 6:9 (AMP)

Challenge Corner

- On a scale of 1-10 (1 being super low and 10 being super high), how would you rate your oomph factor regarding seeking the Lord and His Word?

  1   2   3   4   5   6   7   8   9   10

- What are some practical steps you can take today to begin upping that oomph factor?

_____

_____

_____

_____

_____

_____

_____

_____

- Have you ever lost something; your keys, phone, wallet, remote, only to find it later on? How did you feel after finding that thing? In the same manner, when we seek God with all our hearts, He shows us remarkable things through His Word and gives us awesome opportunities to share the gospel and be an encouragement to others! The feeling we had of finding those keys or wallet wanes in comparison! Therefore, make every effort to seek the Lord today. You won't regret it.

Mornings with Jesus ☀

"SEEK AND YOU SHALL FIND"

W	R	N	E	G	X	F	T	E	C	P	C	Z	F	A	X	I
P	G	N	I	Y	R	R	U	C	S	W	R	G	T	X	M	M
A	Y	R	R	U	C	S	U	W	G	N	O	O	Y	Q	A	Y
E	D	A	H	E	A	P	I	N	G	O	W	S	E	E	K	B
R	A	T	T	L	E	M	L	G	V	Y	D	N	R	E	H	R
S	E	D	I	H	M	R	Z	N	Q	X	S	C	L	P	P	E
N	O	I	S	S	A	P	M	O	C	M	E	E	M	N	M	T
C	Z	C	T	F	E	A	C	V	G	C	C	O	Q	R	S	N
L	Y	T	O	V	C	G	A	B	I	T	O	B	X	A	T	U
E	O	R	R	H	N	N	X	R	T	H	F	F	N	G	O
A	F	E	J	C	A	I	X	I	C	K	D	K	V	E	X	C
R	U	A	W	R	D	T	C	M	J	L	A	O	I	W	N	N
N	D	S	E	A	N	A	M	P	W	E	S	S	Z	V	O	E
I	B	U	J	E	U	L	L	A	R	N	O	T	S	U	G	V
N	P	R	X	S	B	U	S	B	O	O	K	Z	W	D	G	B
G	H	E	F	F	A	M	Y	P	X	U	C	I	U	Q	M	F
J	K	I	H	C	O	E	I	V	H	E	A	R	T	Y	N	W

Seek	Gusto	Scurrying
Search	Ice Cream	Hides
Scurry	Emulating	Treasure
Compassion	Rattle	Heart
Oomph	Electric	Crowds
Abundance	Encounter	Heaping
Learning	Reap	Breakfast

"And whatsoever ye do in word or deed, do all in the name of the Lord Jesus, giving thanks to God and the Father by him." (Colossians 3:17)

We can't give what we don't have.
The only way to give peace
is to first win the war
on the inside of us
through the Word of God
and the power of the
Holy Spirit!

Shortcuts

"Imitate me, just as I imitate Christ."
~I Corinthians 11:1 (AMP)

Something we enjoy doing as a family is playing video games, specifically platforming games, which involves much jumping, quick thinking, and memorization.

Some of the levels get quite difficult because they require you to memorize where certain things are.

One wrong move and it is game over.

One of the best ways to get past these levels is watching each other play, paying close attention where to jump, when to jump, and when and where not to.

I love Jesus!

In our walk with Him, He places people in our lives that we can follow. If we are careful to pay attention to what they do, how they handle certain situations, the habits they hold, and so forth, it will greatly help us, providing special insight into certain situations, and allowing us to gain victory in areas simply because we know what to do and what not to do.

These people serve as God-given shortcuts!

The Bible serves as a major God-given shortcut. It is chock full of people that have done both good and evil things from which we can garner much wisdom, knowing what to do, and what not to do.

Listen, it's important to realize however, that God-given shortcuts never involve compromise.

If the people in our lives are not emulating Jesus, we don't need to and shouldn't follow them.

However, be thankful for the ones who are!

Be encouraged today! Take an assessment of the people in your life right now. Who are the ones who are perhaps further ahead in an area that you are struggling in? What can you learn from them?

Don't worry; a close walk with Jesus will keep us away from compromise.

We are not on this journey alone. We are the Body of Christ.

Who can you learn from today?

_____

_____

_____

_____

_____

_____

_____

_____

Challenge Corner

• What are some examples of God-given shortcuts you can follow?

_____

_____

_____

_____

_____

_____

_____

_____

_____

- Not all shortcuts are created equal! Can you name some that are not good to take?

_____
_____
_____
_____
_____
_____
_____
_____
_____
_____
_____
_____
_____
_____
_____

- Has there been someone in your life that you have looked up to? A role model that you have emulated to help you get further than you would have without them? If so, when was the last time you thanked them? Encouraged them?

_____
_____
_____
_____
_____
_____
_____
_____
_____
_____
_____
_____
_____
_____

- How can you be a positive, Godly example to the people in your life?

_____

_____

_____

_____

_____

_____

_____

_____

_____

_____

_____

_____

_____

_____

_____

_____

_____

_____

_____

_____

_____

_____

_____

"Mark the blameless man,
and observe the upright;
For the future of that man is peace."
~Psalm 37:37 (NKJV)

Mornings with Jesus

"SEEK AND YOU SHALL FIND"

G	M	A	J	O	R	L	R	B	I	F	O	R	N	I	A	G
P	J	S	F	T	I	X	C	X	M	A	J	E	Y	M	Y	P
W	O	I	S	S	C	Z	J	E	I	M	M	V	H	W	P	F
T	U	B	H	I	O	A	H	Z	T	I	T	O	J	X	J	F
H	R	N	O	R	M	D	F	I	A	L	S	E	U	I	Q	Z
W	N	B	R	H	P	Q	L	R	T	Y	E	M	I	K	F	W
R	E	Z	T	C	R	P	N	O	E	A	M	A	F	E	O	B
O	Y	Z	C	F	O	J	E	M	T	S	A	G	D	L	V	L
N	I	G	U	O	M	E	V	E	W	S	G	R	L	D	E	B
G	E	N	T	Y	I	S	I	M	S	E	Z	O	A	I	S	E
M	K	I	S	D	S	U	G	L	M	S	F	R	O	F	R	V
O	S	T	M	O	E	S	D	E	F	S	F	E	X	F	I	I
V	V	A	B	B	R	O	O	A	E	M	W	J	M	I	E	C
E	S	L	S	W	Y	R	G	R	L	E	Y	X	X	C	L	T
I	R	U	B	O	D	N	Q	N	K	N	G	G	X	U	P	O
H	L	M	N	V	D	J	P	O	D	T	Q	G	A	L	S	R
U	U	E	P	A	H	O	I	H	K	L	A	W	S	T	P	Y

Game Over
God Given
Compromise
Follow
Wrong Move
Walk
Emulating

Assessment
Shortcuts
Learn
Jesus
Journey
Major
Victory

Body of Christ
Family
Gain
Difficult
Games
Memorize
Imitate

"Draw nigh to God, and he will draw nigh to you. Cleanse your hands, ye sinners; and purify your hearts, ye double minded."
(James 4:8)

11

Fire, Burn In Me

By: Joshua Scott Zeitz

Fire, burn in me,
burn what I can't see.
I wanna be like Jesus,
I wanna be, free.

Free to fly,
and free to move.
Free to live,
and free to choose.
A slave to sin no longer,
captive to the Hope that He provides!

A war is raging!
Spirit & Soul collide!

I wanna be like Jesus
But am I ready?
To die?

Die to self,
and die to lies?
Die to lust,
and die to pride?

Fire, burn in me!
Burn what I can't see!
I wanna be like Jesus!
I wanna be, clean!

Pure in heart,
and free from greed.
Pure in word,
and pure in deed.

Fire burn in me,
burn what I can't see!
Let the fire of the Word burn in me!

Burn in Me!

"If I say, "I will not remember Him or speak His name anymore," Then my heart becomes a burning fire Shut up in my bones. And I am weary of enduring and holding it in; I cannot endure it [nor contain it any longer]." ~Jeremiah 20:9 (AMP)

We live in uncertain times.

We live in a time when evil is increasingly being called good, and good is being called evil.

We live in a time when it is imperative that we cling to the Word like never before!

We live in a time when the temptation to walk away, to give up on God, on life, on people, on ourselves, on hope, is extremely rampant.

We live in a body and possess a soul that is continually warring against our spirit and the Word of God and, like Paul; we must choose to die daily.

I want to encourage you, fellow saints, to stand strong! Don't give up! Don't give in! You are not alone!

We all struggle with feelings of inadequacy, guilt, shame, pride, jealousy, hurt, loss…

We struggle with sin.

Be encouraged today! The Word is alive, and it works! Let it burn in you today and be encouraged.

Today is simply an encouragement - Don't give up! Keep fighting the good fight of faith! No matter what things look like in the natural, God is on your side. If you are a born-again, Jesus follower, the very gates of Hell cannot stand against you!

Keep letting your light shine!

Let this be your heart's cry today: "Father, let your holy Word burn in me today! Teach me to love the things you love and hate the things you hate."

Challenge Corner

- Life isn't always roses and long walks on the beach. Sometimes the temptation to give up, or to give in, can be quite prevalent. In these times, don't be discouraged. You are not alone! There have been many women and men throughout history who have struggled with this very thing. But remember, even Jesus went through the excruciating feeling of being utterly alone while hanging on the cross, paying the ultimate price for your sin and mine! He cried, "Father, why have you forsaken me!" He suffered that shame so that we would never be alone. Encourage yourself today!

- When was the last time you felt utterly alone? Is this something you struggle with? Perhaps you are in that place now? Perhaps you are in a physical place where you feel alone? A mental place? Whatever the case may be, I encourage you to call upon Jesus. Remember: God is always one worship away!

_____

_____

_____

_____

_____

_____

_____

_____

_____

_____

_____

_____

_____

_____

_____

_____

_____

_____

_____

_____

_____

_____

_____

_____

_____

- Sometimes the Bible will feel like it is burning a hole right through us. At times the conviction it brings can feel unbearable, but remember whatever God reveals, He heals! Therefore, learning to welcome the correction from the Lord, from His Word, will serve to bring about much needed revelation, wisdom, knowledge, and guidance. The ultimate goal is to become more like Jesus in everything we say and do!

- Today has been all about keeping that fire alive in us. Galatians 6:9 challenges us not to grow weary in well-doing. It does that because God is touched with our weaknesses, and He knows the temptations we face, the desire to be reclusive and shut ourselves away, but it's in these moments that we need to draw closer to Him like never before and reach out to people like never before!

Is there a rap, poem, or prayer on your heart today?

_____

_____

_____

_____

_____

_____

_____

_____

_____

_____

_____

_____

_____

_____

_____

_____

_____

_____

_____

_____

_____

_____

_____

_____

We never outgrow the need
for the refiner's fire!

Mornings with Jesus

"SEEK AND YOU SHALL FIND"

O	O	A	T	X	E	L	Y	S	V	N	N	F	S	O	R	V
E	Y	B	C	O	N	T	A	I	N	I	N	G	H	P	D	E
V	B	W	E	A	R	Y	B	A	F	A	K	B	U	J	Q	W
I	W	F	A	I	T	H	P	H	O	T	P	C	Z	F	G	N
T	P	E	U	Z	V	O	W	G	R	R	Y	I	Q	V	O	Z
A	C	C	Z	N	K	W	A	N	S	E	R	L	W	E	C	A
R	W	Y	M	O	W	W	R	I	A	C	J	W	I	O	Y	J
E	B	G	V	I	E	E	R	T	K	N	C	I	N	A	A	I
P	U	U	Z	T	L	V	I	H	E	U	Z	V	E	K	D	N
M	R	E	C	A	L	I	N	G	N	F	I	M	R	C	L	A
I	N	N	Y	T	D	L	G	I	U	C	Q	U	U	U	Q	D
X	I	I	S	P	O	A	K	F	T	C	B	Y	D	F	Q	E
R	N	H	S	M	I	X	Q	I	Z	P	Y	A	N	J	Z	Q
L	M	S	R	E	N	B	O	H	Z	L	L	D	E	P	Q	U
R	E	Y	K	T	G	N	Z	R	F	O	B	O	I	M	N	A
K	Z	G	S	A	I	N	T	S	U	D	I	T	G	N	L	C
G	T	E	A	C	H	X	D	C	Z	H	I	S	T	O	R	Y

Inadequacy	Warring	Daily
Weary	Uncertain	Endure
Temptation	Shine	Well Doing
Faith	History	Saints
Today	Burn In Me	Fighting
Imperative	Conviction	Contain
Forsaken	Alive	Teach

"And I will walk at liberty:
For I seek thy precepts."
(Psalm 119:45)

19

Beyond the Veil
By: Joshua Scott Zeitz

when your prayers don't get answered
the way you want them to
when you feel like you're alone
in what you're going through
the what ifs, the what nows,
the whys, and the worries
the shoulda's, the coulda's,
the memories, the stories
the why them's, the why me's
the why now's, absurd!
though broken
though battered
clinging to His Word!
A Lighthouse in the darkness
A Lamp unto my feet!
when all I see is loss,
when all I feel,
is defeat
Beyond the veil
Sweet Jesus
help me see

Day 34

You Are What You Eat

"Jesus saith unto them, My meat is to do the will of him that sent me, and to finish his work." ~John 4:34 (KJV)

It's good to return to the basics, especially in our walk with the Lord.

Oftentimes as Christians, we tend to want "deep" things, emotionally moving things. We want to "feel" God moving all around us.

Listen, God never changes!

That's awesome news! We may not always feel Him or even sense His presence, but He never changes.

How do we know that? The Bible tells me so!

In John 4, we find the disciples coming back from a food run in a neighboring town, and they are surprised to find Jesus speaking with a Samaritan woman. They are also surprised when they ask Jesus if He has eaten already, because He tells them His food is to do the will of the Father.

Looking only through their natural eyes, they didn't understand the awesome thing that had just occurred between Jesus and the woman, nor did they realize the revival that was about to hit her entire town.

Listen, the Bible keeps us grounded. It keeps us smack dab in the will of God for our lives! It keeps us living with an eternal perspective. It keeps us in a position to be able to minister to others, to share the gospel with them.

The disciples missed an awesome opportunity to experience a

mighty move of God simply because they didn't understand that we are what we eat. Jesus said in Matthew 4:4 that man does not live on bread alone, but on every Word that proceeds from the mouth of God!

Sure, the disciples got to experience the revival because of Jesus and what He did, but wouldn't it be nice if we were the ones to initiate the moves of God in people's lives? Wouldn't it be nice to realize that Jesus said *"Greater things than these shall you do, because I go to the Father"*?

As born-again believers, we have the authority and power on the inside to do mighty things in Jesus' name!

But we have to be willing to be inconvenienced, to walk through crowds slowly, to miss a meal here or there, miss an appointment perhaps that can easily be rescheduled later.

We are what we eat and, just like Jesus, our first meat should be to do the will of our Father.

Don't be afraid to ask God today to help you see and take advantage of divine opportunities!

Challenge Corner

- Read John 4 today. How did Jesus deal with this woman? How did he deal with her sin? How did he meet her right where she was? How can we carry this into our lives?

_____

_____

_____

_____

_____

_____

_____

_____

_____

_____

- It's very easy to point the finger at everyone else, finding fault in what they are doing and saying. BUT it's far better for us to realize that we are what we eat, and to work out our own salvation with fear and trembling. What are some things the Lord has been dealing with you about lately?

_____

_____

_____

_____

_____

_____

_____

_____

_____

_____

_____

_____

_____

_____

_____

_____

_____

_____

_____

_____

_____

_____

_____

_____

_____

_____

_____

_____

_____

_____

- In light of the truth above, "we are what we eat," what are some practical steps we can take to begin eating better things? To better equip us to have a closer walk with Jesus, to better be able to reach others with the Good News? (Hint: whatever we are full of is going to come spilling out in our speech and actions. If we are full of the Word, this will come out. Likewise, if we are full of fear, gossip, or worry, that will come out.) What do you want to be full of?

_____

_____

_____

_____

_____

_____

_____

_____

_____

_____

_____

_____

_____

_____

_____

_____

_____

_____

_____

_____

_____

_____

_____

_____

Mornings with Jesus

"SEEK AND YOU SHALL FIND"

F	R	I	N	C	O	N	V	E	N	I	E	N	C	E	D	O
B	N	N	O	F	G	Q	D	U	X	S	N	O	I	T	C	A
A	E	U	M	L	X	H	W	E	I	L	T	X	H	J	R	T
S	R	E	W	O	P	P	O	O	D	L	B	O	N	S	G	A
I	W	C	G	O	S	P	E	L	W	N	A	V	L	A	E	M
C	O	A	K	Z	Z	Z	D	R	X	Q	U	V	N	D	H	M
S	K	J	Q	L	B	I	T	A	S	I	J	O	I	E	C	V
U	Z	Q	E	C	V	H	F	X	U	P	T	P	R	V	E	J
B	D	E	S	I	R	P	R	U	S	T	E	M	I	G	E	I
B	U	Y	N	H	M	B	F	L	C	R	H	C	F	W	P	R
H	D	E	L	U	D	E	H	C	S	E	R	O	T	E	S	H
O	A	P	P	O	I	N	T	M	E	N	T	S	R	I	S	Z
U	A	T	U	W	S	S	F	I	N	I	S	H	S	I	V	U
N	C	I	W	I	D	N	O	I	T	A	V	L	A	S	T	E
E	S	N	E	S	A	Z	K	B	S	U	O	O	O	M	X	Y
K	Y	T	D	A	E	R	B	S	A	M	A	R	I	T	A	N
L	B	R	I	O	P	P	O	R	T	U	N	I	T	I	E	S

Basics	Finish	Speech
Surprised	Samaritan	Divine
Sense	Revival	Inconvenienced
Appointment	Power	Grounded
Rescheduled	Opportunities	Actions
Meal	Salvation	Bread
Authority	Gospel	Perspective

"I sought the LORD, and he heard me, And delivered me from all my fears." (Psalm 34:4)

Toothaches & Birthdays

Have you ever had a toothache or some other great physical pain?

At the moment, it feels like the most excruciating thing ever, with no end in sight!

BUT eventually the pain subsides, and the memory of that pain fades into oblivion.

The Bible says our life is but a vapor, here today and gone tomorrow.

In short, life goes by so fast!

Taking advantage of the time we have, redeeming that time, making the most of it, is so very important.

Recently, I was at an event where I was surrounded by amazing friends & awesome food. It was a birthday party for the ages! After getting home from the party, I told my wife, "This is the kind of party you wish you could just do all over again - the type of party that doesn't happen very often!"

There will come a time when all we will have left is what we have given away, what we have purposefully sowed into the people around us.

The older I get, the more I have come to realize how much relationships matter. People matter!

God designed it that way! We weren't created to be alone or isolated. We were designed to interact with one another, to connect, to reach out, to be givers, to be like God!

It's in this place of intimacy with the Lord where we can truly flourish and shine bright!

Listen, toothaches are horrible, but the pain will fade. Birthday parties are great, but they, too, end.

However, relationships can last a lifetime and the things we do and say within those relationships can have an eternal impact!

Be thankful for the friends you have! The people in your life that love you and truly care for you!

It can be so easy and tempting to focus only on what you don't have and miss all the wonderful blessings you do!

Be encouraged today. Birthday parties and toothaches produce very different results, but both are just temporary. But the things we do with and for the Lord, for others, will last for eternity!

Challenge Corner

- Name an event or occurrence in your life, whether good or bad, that felt at the time like it was the best or worst thing ever.

_____

_____

_____

_____

_____

_____

_____

_____

_____

_____

_____

_____

No matter how good or bad the thing was, it's over now...for better or worse.

- Life is short. What are some practical things or steps you can take today to make the most of the time you have been given?

_____

_____

_____

_____

_____

_____

_____

_____

_____

_____

_____

_____

_____

_____

- What does it mean to redeem our time?

_____

_____

_____

_____

_____

_____

_____

_____

_____

_____

_____

_____

_____

_____

- God is masterful at redeeming our time. He can do in a moment what we cannot do in an entire lifetime! Let Him know today what He means to you!

_____

_____

_____

_____

_____

_____

_____

_____

_____

_____

_____

_____

_____

_____

_____

_____

_____

_____

_____

_____

_____

_____

_____

_____

Feelings and experiences
come and go like the wind,
but the Word of God will remain forever!

Is there a rap, poem, or prayer on your heart today?

_____
_____
_____
_____
_____
_____
_____
_____
_____
_____
_____
_____
_____
_____
_____
_____
_____
_____
_____
_____
_____
_____
_____
_____
_____
_____
_____
_____
_____
_____

Mornings with Jesus

"SEEK AND YOU SHALL FIND"

A	E	O	M	J	V	N	E	S	K	D	Q	Y	G	R	T	U
P	X	W	J	J	V	B	O	N	E	E	A	B	E	S	C	R
B	C	O	U	I	Y	W	I	S	A	E	E	L	X	R	A	E
N	R	N	P	E	E	S	I	R	E	H	A	Y	W	E	R	T
D	U	D	L	D	T	G	K	D	T	T	K	M	W	V	E	T
E	C	E	T	C	N	E	I	C	I	H	I	E	Q	I	T	A
T	I	R	G	E	B	S	R	O	Q	L	D	U	S	G	N	M
A	A	F	D	S	B	N	N	N	M	C	B	A	F	G	I	N
L	T	U	I	U	R	S	I	N	A	G	X	B	Y	G	S	R
O	I	L	S	Z	H	E	W	E	T	L	S	X	Y	S	E	E
S	N	K	A	I	L	H	E	C	H	I	L	Z	S	P	I	D
I	G	R	P	P	S	N	Y	T	N	T	M	Y	C	U	T	E
W	F	S	O	U	O	V	V	F	E	X	E	E	F	L	R	E
V	L	E	D	L	L	I	F	E	T	I	M	E	K	H	A	M
F	P	X	A	N	V	H	R	G	F	D	J	Q	O	U	P	I
J	E	O	D	C	S	E	H	C	A	H	T	O	O	T	E	N
B	E	A	X	S	U	N	W	C	W	F	O	O	D	D	G	G

Excruciating
Birthdays
Interact
Redeeming
Connect
Relationships
People

Toothaches
Sowed
Eternally
Time
Parties
Matter
Wonderful

Isolated
Food
Lifetime
Designed
Subside
Givers
Alone

"Trust in the LORD with all thine heart; And lean not unto thine own understanding. In all thy ways acknowledge him, And he shall direct thy paths."
(Proverbs 3:5,6)

Short

(Written in honor of Jo Annette Lopez)
By: Joshua Scott Zeitz

Life is so short,
God, help me see what matters!
Hand to the plow,
Steady climbin up these ladders!
Chasin fame, seekin names,
Got my life all in tatters!
Chasin thrills, seekin frills,
Got me hangin from the rafters!
Money on my mind,
But no thought to what comes after!
Steady livin for the now,
But this is just a chapter!
Word to your mama,
Mine went home to be with Jesus,
Life is more than pleasure,
Steady seekin things that please us!
We only get one life,
It's time to make it count!
I'm layin down my pride,
And everything that leads to drought!

Dry bones come alive!
Sin put my life in squalor,
Forgiven, freed, and focused,
Steady quenched from Living Water!
Empty, hurt, and broken?!
Be freed in Jesus' name!
Believe the gospel spoken,
You'll never be the same!
Listen!
This world is atrocious,
it eats you up for sport,
For God so loved the world,
the time is now,
Life is short!

"For God so loved the world,
He gave His only begotten Son,
that whosoever, believes on Him,
would not perish,
but have everlasting life!"
~John 3:16 (KJV)

More Word, Less Me

"But what things were gain to me, these I have counted loss for Christ." ~Philippians 3:7 (NKJV)

We are living in some crazy times! Do you realize the Apostle Paul was living during some crazy times as well? Do you realize that ever since sin entered the world, crazy times have been prevalent?

Sin always brings death. Death always means separation, separation from a loving Father. Therefore, wherever sin is allowed to run rampant, so too, darkness is going to run rampant.

To try to counteract the effects of sin in any way other than with the Word is futile. This is why it is so important that we as Christians delve into the Word in these last days like never before!

We are living in a time of gross darkness and the only thing to dispel it is the Word!

"Thy word is a lamp unto my feet, and a light unto my path." ~Psalm 119:105 (KJV)

The apostle Paul was an awesome man of God, but he knew that without Christ, he was lost!

"Brethren, I count not myself to have apprehended: but this one thing I do, forgetting those things which are behind, and reaching forth unto those things which are before, I press toward the mark for the prize of the high calling of God in Christ Jesus." ~Philippians 3:13-14 (KJV)

Listen, when life kicks our bucket, whatever's on the inside, in abundance, is going to spill out!

What do you want to spill out, you or the Word? I say we rise up a standard in these last days and allow the Word to come out!

Why is this so important?

"But if our gospel be hid, it is hid to them that are lost: In whom the god of this world hath blinded the minds of them which believe not, lest the light of the glorious gospel of Christ, who is the image of God, should shine unto them."
~II Corinthians 4:3-4 (KJV)

The enemy is working overtime to keep his followers blinded to the Truth, to the Light!

There is no reasoning with sin. There is no reasoning with death. There is no reasoning with darkness. There is One answer and One alone: His name is Jesus!

It is imperative that we not only allow Him to have the throne of our hearts always, but that we fill up on Him every day! There is a real devil out there. He is a defeated foe. He is a conquered foe. But he will still, as I once heard a pastor say, "Eat your lunch and pop the bag," if we let him.

Let's not let him! Let's be full of the Word! Not only for ourselves, but for a world that is lost, hurting, and blind! They need Jesus, not vain philosophy. They need Jesus, not vain initiatives. They need Jesus, not temporary fixes. They need Jesus, not one-liners, memes, or gifs.

What do you say, fellow soul winner? Let this be our motto in these last days, "More Word, Less Me!"

Challenge Corner

- Devotionals can be tricky things. Why? Namely, because if we aren't careful they will keep us focused on ourselves only. There comes a time, however, when we must reach out to others using the things we have been learning in these devotionals! In other words, unless we give away what we have freely been given, we simply become "spiritually fat!"

- Who in your life right now could use an encouraging Word? Perhaps they just need someone to write them a letter, fix them a meal, or give them a hug? Whatever it is and whoever it is, perhaps you are the one to provide it today! There is no greater feeling on earth than being the answer to prayer for someone else!

_____

_____

_____

_____

_____

_____

_____

_____

_____

_____

_____

_____

_____

_____

_____

_____

_____

_____

_____

_____

_____

_____

_____

- Seek the Lord today. Ask Him how you can be a blessing to someone else. Write down their names and begin praying for them. Watch, wait, and listen. The Lord will speak to you, so be ready!

Mornings with Jesus

"SEEK AND YOU SHALL FIND"

P	K	T	E	M	P	O	R	A	R	Y	P	D	Y	R	S	D
G	C	R	N	A	O	S	R	H	X	E	E	G	A	F	C	E
U	T	N	E	L	A	V	E	R	P	D	P	M	R	H	V	D
S	B	A	K	T	F	H	U	Q	N	D	P	Y	B	W	V	N
L	P	M	B	Z	U	E	M	I	R	A	K	I	C	K	S	E
A	O	N	U	D	H	Q	L	A	N	Q	Q	I	B	E	E	H
N	P	D	D	N	X	B	W	T	X	D	U	W	R	M	R	E
O	T	R	A	V	C	O	U	N	T	E	D	J	M	S	E	R
I	H	O	N	S	T	F	E	L	T	S	O	P	A	S	A	P
T	E	W	S	S	G	Y	S	T	P	L	T	B	S	E	S	P
O	B	E	W	E	F	P	S	G	H	P	E	D	E	L	O	A
V	A	R	E	R	N	R	E	R	T	P	K	J	U	C	N	W
E	G	O	R	P	G	A	N	P	M	R	C	K	E	Z	I	S
D	S	M	E	E	H	Y	K	Z	V	I	U	Z	H	O	N	F
O	B	F	D	O	Q	E	R	W	Y	Z	B	W	X	U	G	T
P	C	C	H	B	G	R	A	P	Z	E	Q	L	I	L	M	J
Z	A	Y	I	U	D	W	D	Z	L	F	O	T	T	O	M	I

Apprehended	Bucket	Reasoning
Counted	Darkness	Answered
Kicks	Apostle	Temporary
More Word	Pop the Bag	Devotionals
Less Me	Press	Blinded
Rampant	Toward	Motto
Prevalent	Prize	Prayer

"Finally, my brethren, be strong in the Lord, and in the power of his might."
(Ephesians 6:10)

Off With Their Heads!

By: Joshua Scott Zeitz

Imagine living in a world without hopes or
dreams...
Ain't gotta travel far,
don't need no time machine.
These first world problems,
a deplorable scene!
Lil' Timmy lost his daddy,
and his mama's a fiend!
But we're too busy building churches,
pack'em in like sardines!
Hand a pamphlet, pat a back,
get'em on our routine!
Hand-feeding them that milk,
don't want to see them get weaned!
If they think for themselves,
Go and grab the guillotine!
It's off with their heads,
cause they're just blockin' the screen!

Pure Heart, Pure Mind

"Blessed are the pure in heart: for they shall see God."
~Matthew 5:8 (KJV)

Ever heard someone say something like this "You know, God works in mysterious ways!"

While this may sound good, it isn't entirely true. Why? We serve a God who wants us to be as close to Him as we can be! We serve a God who longs to give us the inside scoop! Why? Because He loves us!

All throughout the Old Testament, Christ can be seen. All throughout the Old Testament, the Bible points to the coming Christ, how He would suffer, die, and redeem us back to God. Then, when Jesus showed up, He pointed to the same thing; how He would suffer, die, and be raised from the dead, and how He would ascend to Heaven, send the Holy Spirit, and so forth.

All throughout the scriptures, we find God wanting to let mankind in on His plan, but we also find that oftentimes people can't see it, can't perceive it. Why? Because they are blind to it, focusing on other things instead.

Today I want to encourage you! I want you and me to see just how good God is and how much He so desires to let us in on His inner workings!

Check out these awesome passages:

"But as it is written, Eye hath not seen, nor ear heard, neither have entered into the heart of man, the things that God hath prepared for them that love him. But God hath revealed them unto us by his Spirit: for the Spirit searcheth all things, yea the deep things of God. For what man

knoweth the things of a man, save the spirit of man which is in him? Even so the things of God knoweth no man, but the Spirit of God.

Now we have received, not the spirit of the world, but the spirit which is of God; that we might know the things that are freely given to us of God.

For who knoweth the mind of the Lord, that he may instruct him? <u>But we have the mind of Christ.</u>"
~I Corinthians 2:9-12 & 16 (KJV)

I would encourage you to read the entirety of this passage a few times over!

Listen, God isn't the "old man upstairs," or some uncaring entity out of touch with His creation! He is a good God, and He wants to fellowship with us, letting us in on His plans on the earth! In fact, many of His overall big-picture plans, He has already revealed to us in the scriptures.

As for everyday life, He longs for us to walk with Him and talk with Him! He wants us on the inside!

How do we do this?

Simply put, by having a pure heart.

"Wherewithal shall a young man cleanse his way? By taking heed thereto according to thy word. With my whole heart have I sought thee: O let me not wander from thy commandments." ~Psalm 119:9-10 (KJV)

When we seek the Lord with all our hearts, we will find Him. When we intentionally put Him first in our day, in our week, in our home, in our business, in our everyday life, He will show up in a mighty way, giving us insight that we never thought possible!

He will enable us to see and do things that we never thought possible. We will be privy to His plans, His ways, and we will do mighty things for Him and through Him!

Be encouraged today! We serve a God who is ever-present, who longs to be intimate with us, be affectionate with us, and who longs to freely give to us, so that we can freely give to others!

Challenge Corner

- Have you ever seen God as "the man upstairs" type or as some unreachable entity? Do you still?

_____

_____

_____

_____

- How *do* you see God?

_____

_____

_____

_____

_____

_____

_____

_____

_____

_____

_____

_____

_____

_____

_____

_____

_____

_____

_____

_____

_____

_____

_____

- Based on what we have learned throughout this devotional, how can we both fear God (Reverence Him in Holy Worship) and approach Him boldly as a loving Heavenly Father?

_____

_____

_____

_____

_____

_____

_____

_____

_____

_____

_____

_____

_____

_____

_____

_____

_____

_____

_____

_____

_____

- We haven't all had the best relationships with our earthly fathers, nor have we all had the best encounters with people of authority. This can carry over into our relationship with God if we let it. But please don't be deceived. God is not like any earthly father or any earthly authoritative figure, even the really good ones! He is oh so much better! He always disciplines us for our benefit, corrects us to bring us closer to Him, and convicts us to keep us from sin. And He always desires to fellowship with us, to see us free from harm, danger, and evil. He is a good, good Father.

Mornings with Jesus

"SEEK AND YOU SHALL FIND"

U	T	X	B	C	O	R	R	E	C	T	S	E	K	O	F	A
G	W	A	O	T	X	U	T	E	S	F	P	V	W	R	Y	Z
W	C	S	B	I	M	V	S	P	T	T	R	S	J	X	R	X
V	D	B	E	F	V	E	I	S	N	E	V	E	Z	T	S	A
P	E	M	R	E	X	Y	R	N	E	V	W	U	C	H	M	T
R	C	E	U	N	Y	I	H	M	M	E	K	C	E	G	E	S
I	E	V	P	E	H	W	C	A	D	R	T	S	S	I	E	O
V	I	E	B	B	Y	E	F	N	N	P	L	E	N	S	D	M
Y	V	R	I	B	J	C	O	U	A	R	D	R	E	N	E	T
L	E	Y	N	E	C	N	D	P	M	E	E	R	T	I	R	U
R	D	D	G	W	L	E	N	S	M	S	V	J	S	E	U	R
D	V	A	Y	Y	E	R	I	T	O	E	I	J	I	F	U	P
N	Q	Y	S	H	A	E	M	A	C	N	E	Q	L	K	O	G
E	P	U	T	D	N	V	T	I	C	T	C	J	V	O	Q	L
O	N	A	H	F	S	E	H	R	H	Z	E	S	C	T	O	T
B	R	L	X	U	E	R	R	S	T	Q	R	S	V	L	Q	U
W	C	Y	T	I	T	N	E	Y	M	B	L	T	Q	B	K	V

Received	Mind of Christ	Benefit
Everyday	Ever Present	Rescues
Pure	Cleanse	Reverence
Commandments	Deceived	Entity
Scoop	Man Upstairs	Listens
Wrath	Utmost	Insight
Privy	Redeems	Corrects

"And be not conformed to this world: but be ye transformed by the renewing of your mind, that ye may prove what is that good, and acceptable, and perfect, will of God."
(Romans 12:2)

43

Sold Out

By: Joshua Scott Zeitz

Been servin God,
but am I servin the people?
Sold out to the cause,
or a slave to the steeple?
Seekin titles, like bishop and apostle?
Preachin good works,
instead of preachin the gospel?
You know how it is,
gimmehollywood Jesus,
pretty hair, soulful flair,
and mantras that tease us!
Never warn about Hell,
only sing about Heaven,
Jesus be my guide?
More like lucky number 7!
My best life now,
livin life for the moment,
I got these first world problems...
should I rent it? or own it?

Kids hooked on porn,
I got a three-car garage!
Postin selfies on my social,
gotta boost this mirage!
An illusionist.
Bank's in the black,
but I'm losin it.
Alarms goin off,
but I'm snoozin it!
It's time for honesty,
I stopped seekin.
Set to cruise control,
and I've been sleepin.
It's time for change.
It's time for purpose.
I got these castles in the sand,
but they're empty and worthless!
Life's in the red
By the blood of the Lamb,
I've been purchased!
Sold out,
not just surface!

God is Good!

"O taste and see that the Lord is good: blessed is the man that trusteth in him." ~Psalms 34:8 (KJV)

Getting to know the Lord is one of the most awesome things!

The "Good News" is this: We can get as close to God as we want!

He designed it that way. He is not some uncaring, unfeeling, tyrant in the air.

"For we do not have a High Priest who is unable to sympathize and understand our weaknesses and temptations, but One who has been tempted [knowing exactly how it feels to be human] *in every respect as we are, yet without* [committing any] *sin. Therefore, let us* [with privilege] *approach the throne of grace* [that is, the throne of God's gracious favor] *with confidence and without fear, so that we may receive mercy* [for our failures] *and find* [His amazing] *grace to help in time of need* [an appropriate blessing, coming just at the right moment]."*
~Hebrews 4:15-16 (AMP)

Learning to trust God will elevate our walk with Him in a magnificent way. Knowing that He cares for us, that He wants the best for us, that He desires to see us grow, prosper, and thrive, this will cause us to want to serve Him, to want to tell others about Him!

Suddenly, life becomes a "get to" and not a "have to."

Listen, the Bible is our number one way to get to know Him more. The more we not only read it, but adhere to it, obey it, cherish it, desire it, the more we will see Jesus portrayed throughout it and we will find that God has been there all along calling people to Himself!

Calling us to Himself!

He is a good God!

I cannot stress this enough, because until we realize He is for us and not against us, we are going to have a difficult time fully trusting Him, fully surrendering to Him.

Today, I want to encourage you to think about all the things He has done for you, in you, and through you! Write them down.

On our journey to know Him more, it's imperative that we learn to trust Him, trust His Word, and realize He is good—all the time.

Challenge Corner

- What is your view of God? We have touched on this already in previous questions, but it's vital that you have a clear grasp of your view! You see, how we view God will ultimately be how we view life and how we view people and relationships as well. If our view of God is skewed, if we think He is some mean man upstairs, or that He is causing and giving His stamp of approval to the atrocities around the world, we are going to have a difficult time sharing Him with others!

_____

_____

_____

_____

_____

_____

_____

_____

_____

_____

_____

_____

_____

_____

_____

_____

- Why is it so important to spend time in the Word of God?

_____
_____
_____
_____
_____
_____
_____
_____
_____
_____
_____
_____
_____

- What does the Word of God mean to you?

_____
_____
_____
_____
_____
_____
_____
_____
_____
_____
_____
_____
_____
_____
_____
_____

- Do you see the Word of God as the final authority?

_____
_____
_____
_____
_____
_____
_____
_____
_____
_____
_____
_____
_____
_____
_____
_____

- Do you hold the Word of God in high esteem or do you see it as simply another book to bring a semblance of comfort and peace?

_____
_____
_____
_____
_____
_____
_____
_____
_____
_____
_____
_____
_____
_____
_____
_____
_____

Is there a rap, poem, or prayer on your heart today?

_____
_____
_____
_____
_____
_____
_____
_____
_____
_____
_____
_____
_____
_____
_____
_____
_____
_____
_____
_____
_____
_____
_____
_____
_____
_____

"Every good gift and every perfect gift is from above, and comes down from the Father of lights, with whom there is no variation or shadow of turning." ~James 1:17 (NKJV)

Mornings with Jesus

"SEEK AND YOU SHALL FIND"

S	Q	Q	O	T	N	E	C	I	F	I	N	G	A	M	E	W
Y	C	V	U	D	Q	Q	P	A	S	E	T	A	V	E	L	E
M	V	G	S	Y	S	R	E	P	E	R	T	O	I	R	E	C
P	L	D	O	O	S	U	R	R	E	N	D	E	R	I	N	G
A	Q	B	E	D	E	G	T	V	I	T	A	L	N	E	M	H
T	M	B	O	Y	I	U	O	B	D	E	N	G	I	S	E	D
H	S	C	R	B	A	S	J	P	B	I	B	L	E	F	B	Q
I	G	O	R	Y	B	R	G	N	I	A	G	A	N	R	O	B
Z	T	E	J	F	T	E	T	O	K	W	N	G	Z	O	K	Y
E	A	C	O	C	Y	M	O	R	O	Q	I	H	W	E	A	P
D	B	G	U	H	R	E	E	U	O	D	Z	W	T	W	A	T
V	I	P	R	E	A	E	L	X	S	P	V	M	E	R	K	G
D	B	E	N	R	N	T	B	N	O	M	E	S	I	D	O	T
P	U	Y	E	I	T	S	W	E	L	R	O	C	M	S	A	W
W	Z	F	Y	S	H	E	J	D	R	M	X	K	A	S	D	M
F	H	C	F	H	B	T	C	K	E	A	S	Q	T	R	I	R
E	V	I	T	A	R	E	P	M	I	S	L	E	Y	X	G	M

Journey	Worth	Born Again
Taste	Elevate	Grace
Imperative	Magnificent	Awesome
Bread	Designed	Esteem
Sympathize	Tyrant	Vital
Repertoire	God is Good	Cherish
Bible	Surrendering	Portrayed

"Then Peter said unto them, Repent, and be baptized every one of you in the name of Jesus Christ for the remission of sins, and ye shall receive the gift of the Holy Ghost."
(Acts 2:38)

Eternity is Calling

By: Joshua Scott Zeitz

In our highs and our lows,
In times of despair and times of rejoicing,

It shows no partiality,
It plays no favorites,

To the rich and to the poor,
To the healthy and to the sick,

To the believers and the doubters,
To the planners and the free spirits,

To the hopeful, and the hopeless,
To the fathered, and the the orphans,

To the privileged and the homeless,
To the lost and the found,

On stormy days and sunny days,
On mountain tops and ocean fronts,

On holy hills, in sinful slums,
On religious days, at pagan parties,

To the devout and disciplined,
To the willful and proud,
To the humble and broken,
To the lonely in crowds,

From age to age,
To every nation and tribe,
His call remains constant,
Eternal life!

Eternity is calling,
He has a name!
To the whosoever,
His call remains the same!

Eternity is calling,
And that is why we go!
To tell about Jesus,
To bring them Hope!

The time is now!
There's no time for stalling,
The world needs Jesus!
Eternity is calling!

"And this is life eternal, that they might know thee the only true God, and Jesus Christ, whom thou hast sent."
~John 17:3 (KJV)

Renewing Your Mind

"And be not conformed to this world: but be ye transformed by the renewing of your mind, that ye may prove what is that good, and acceptable, and perfect, will of God."
~Romans 12:2 (KJV)

"(For the weapons of our warfare are not carnal, but mighty through God to the pulling down of strongholds;) Casting down imaginations, and every high thing that exalteth itself against the knowledge of God, and bringing into captivity every thought to the obedience of Christ;"
~II Corinthians 10:4-5 (KJV)

"Set your mind and keep focused habitually on the things above [the heavenly things], *not on things that are on the earth* [which have only temporal value]. *For you died* [to this world], *and your* [new, real] *life is hidden with Christ in God."*
~Colossians 3:2-3 (AMP)

As born-again believers, we have been redeemed from the curse that still resides on this world.

That's awesome news! However, the enemy wants to keep us bound to our past mistakes, our past sins, and our past selves. The way to overcome this is by renewing our minds to the Word of God!

I am a new creation! *"Old things have passed away, behold all things have become new!"* ~II Corinthians 5:17 (NKJV)

"There is therefore now no condemnation to them which are in Christ Jesus who walk not after the flesh but after the spirit!" ~Romans 8:1 (KJV)

When we speak the Word of God, it releases the power of God in our lives! It reminds the enemy that we are no longer his. It reminds us that we have been made new. It reminds the world that we are different!

Simply speaking the Word, however, is not enough, we must allow it to wash over us to the point that we don't simply speak it from rote memorization, but from a place of faith, of trust, of knowing that we know that it works and that it is our sword!

Listen, the Bible is alive! It works. It is spirit and it is truth. It has the power to change us from the inside out, to bring us into a deeper, more intimate walk with the Lord. It has the power to mold us into a force to be reckoned with!

When we are full of the Word of God, we have the power to cast down wicked imaginations and everything that would dare exalt itself against the knowledge of God!

We live in a world that is anti-Christ, anti-Bible, and anti-Jesus, but can I tell you some more great news?! That doesn't have to faze us when our hope is not in what we can see but what we can't see! The Bible allows us to see the unseen, to have an eternal perspective, to see as God sees, to love as God loves, and to hate as God hates!

With the Bible as our sole guide, we can know Him more, and we can become more like Him!

Be encouraged today, no matter what you are facing right now. The Bible has the answers! Jesus is the answer!

The Bible says, *"For in Him we live and move and exist* [that is, in Him we actually have our being], *as even some of your own poets have said, 'For we also are His children.'"*
~Acts 17:28 (AMP)

In Him we are more than conquerors! In Him we are victorious! In Him we have peace and joy!

He is for you!

If you are struggling today with understanding how much He loves you, if you are struggling with thoughts that are tearing you away from a God who is madly in love with you, if you are struggling with thoughts that are keeping you bound in sin, worry, doubt, fear, and the like - run to Him! Run to the Bible, it is our safe haven, our refuge! Renew your mind to its truths and allow it to wash over you, to heal you, and to speak to you.

If you aren't struggling, if you find yourself in a place where you feel good about life, about God, run to Him! Run to the Bible!

Remember: Getting to know Him more is a life-long pursuit.

Challenge Corner

- Why is it important to renew our minds?

_____

_____

_____

_____

_____

_____

_____

_____

_____

- What does it mean when the Bible says our life is hidden in Christ?

_____

_____

_____

_____

_____

_____

_____

_____

- Speaking the Word, meditating on the Word, this isn't about mind tricks, it's about getting the Word down into our hearts until it permeates our very being. It's about knowing that we know that we know that we know. Listen, there are so many lies out there telling us so many different things. Knowing the Truth for ourselves is imperative if we are going to live a life that is hidden in Christ, one that is ready to serve others and share with others the hope that can only be found in Jesus!

> *"And this is eternal life, that they may know You, the only true God, and Jesus Christ whom You have sent."*
> *~John 17:3 (NKJV)*

God's Love
By: Moriah Rachel Zeitz

We serve an amazing God! The Bible says, "His mercies are new every morning!" (See Lamentations 3:22-23) But even greater than that, and that's pretty great, is his love for us. It says in John 3:16, *"For God so the loved world that he gave His only begotten Son."* God loved you so much that he came to earth to live and die as a lowly human, so we wouldn't have to be separated from him anymore. How amazing is that!

It says in Hebrews 12:2, *"For the joy set before him he endured the cross."* Even in the midst of his suffering, Jesus had such great love for you, for we were the joy set before him! To him, all his pain and agony, not only in his death, but his life on earth as well, was worth it, just to be able to have a relationship with you. Wow, that blows my mind! God's greatest desire is to have your love! To have a relationship with you!

Think about that, God, I mean God himself, the One who created all of life in six days, who showed His marvellous wonders in Egypt and parted the Red Sea, the same God that came to earth as a human and was born of a virgin, who made the deaf to hear, lame to walk, blind to see, and dumb to speak, wants to have a relationship with you! The same God who did so many wonders that it says in John 21:25, *"And there are also many other things that Jesus did, which if they were written one by one, I suppose that even the world itself could not contain the books that would be written."*

That same God's greatest desire is to simply have your love. Isn't that awesome!! I mean who does that!? Nobody but our God does that. For God does not simply love, He is love. His love for you is so great that we aren't even able with our tiny human minds to comprehend the amount of love he has for us!

God loves you so much, and He can't wait for you to wake up in the morning and talk to Him. He can't wait for you to obey Him, so He can bless you beyond measure. If He loves you that much, then we should love Him back with all that we have. Even though our love is but dust in comparison to His, in His eyes, it means all of the world!

Be encouraged today! We don't need to live this life alone. We have a God who desperately wants our attention and love. The Bible says in Joshua that God is a jealous God. He wants to be the centre of your attention, and He wants to be in constant fellowship with His children! So, let's start today by taking time out of our lives to spend a little more time with Jesus.

Challenge Corner

- Do you struggle to spend extra time with God? If so, what is something practical you can do to make it a habit?

_____

_____

_____

_____

_____

_____

_____

_____

_____

_____

_____

_____

_____

- Is there something that you give more attention to, than you give to God? Are you willing to give it up, or put it down to spending some extra time with Him?

_____

_____

_____

_____

_____

_____

_____

_____

_____

_____

_____

_____

_____

_____

_____

_____

_____

_____

_____

_____

_____

_____

_____

_____

_____

_____

_____

_____

_____

_____

_____

_____

Mornings with Jesus ☀

"SEEK AND YOU SHALL FIND"

A	T	R	V	S	L	C	U	R	S	E	F	A	W	O	J	D
J	P	E	W	Y	M	A	N	I	F	E	S	T	S	I	M	H
L	Y	D	T	J	N	Y	C	B	A	L	H	R	P	Z	A	I
V	S	E	E	D	F	V	I	T	I	A	R	T	R	O	P	H
K	N	E	M	Z	Z	R	L	S	N	O	P	A	E	W	G	Q
D	O	M	P	I	Y	D	S	R	O	R	E	U	Q	N	O	C
D	I	E	O	O	N	E	D	D	I	H	J	I	Q	G	X	R
C	T	D	R	Q	J	M	T	E	O	P	X	U	Y	P	D	E
I	A	G	A	B	U	L	R	N	M	E	D	H	A	U	B	N
Z	N	R	L	K	A	W	M	O	M	V	P	L	X	R	R	E
C	I	I	N	X	E	N	L	O	F	O	L	Q	A	S	E	W
E	G	X	E	A	I	Z	C	E	S	R	S	Z	C	U	N	I
W	A	J	B	W	L	R	A	O	I	K	E	X	J	I	N	N
C	M	O	K	Q	E	A	L	F	C	O	E	P	I	T	I	G
J	I	G	J	V	L	I	V	I	Y	H	L	T	T	G	J	J
S	S	G	O	W	H	E	R	A	F	R	A	W	O	U	X	F
H	E	X	F	P	P	T	I	Z	D	X	C	U	O	R	O	Y

Renewing	Warfare	Inner
Temporal	Curse	Tricks
Weapons	Imaginations	Pursuit
Redeemed	Portrait	Hidden
Overcome	Carnal	Conquerors
Exalt	Manifest	Philosophy
Outperform	Rote	Faze

"And this is life eternal,
that they might know thee
the only true God, and
Jesus Christ, whom thou
hast sent."
(John 17:3)

Bursts of Heaven

By: Joshua Scott Zeitz

A cool breeze on a hot day,
A U-turn on a wrong way,
A sun's ray when the sky's gray,
An all-clear on an x-ray,
A scenic walk on a Segway,
A home run from a foul play,
A red rose in a boquet,
A doggy bag when you can't stay,
A paid-in-full when you can't pay,
A vaca on a Monday,
A weekend on a Thursday,
A green light on a straightaway,
A clear lane on the beltway,
Answered prayer when they strayed away,
An overturn from a replay,
A perfect rise on a souffle,
A roll of quarters in the ashtray,
A call from God when you can't pray,
A favorite food on a buffet,

A getaway in a chalet,
An invite to a soiree,
A hotel with a valet,
A new pair when your socks fray,
A buzzer beater from a fadeaway,
An extra hour when you laid awake ,
An extra slice of a b-day cake,
An affirmation when you feel fake,
A forgive when it's your mistake,
A helping hand like shake & bake,
That's old school, make no mistake,
An open door when you can't escape,
A shortcut when you're running late,
An extend on that due date,
An extra squeeze of that Colgate,
An "I do" from your helpmate,
These Bursts of Heaven do feel great!
Got one?
Then fill the blank _____!

Jesus Loves Me, This I Know!

"On that [same] *day, when evening had come, He said to them, "Let us go over to the other side* [of the Sea of Galilee].*""*
~Mark 4:35 (AMP)

There are times when I read things in the Bible and it truly tests my mettle, especially in regard to Jesus and His disciples.

It's easy to sit on this side of things and criticize the disciples for their lack of faith, yelling at the Bible, telling them to go this way or that, as if what we have to say is going to change what has already been done. Better yet, as if, when placed in similar circumstances, we would make the right choices every time!

Today's reading is one of those instances when I am so glad for the Lord's long suffering towards me, His gracious lovingkindness, His love, and His willingness to be the author and finisher of my faith!

Mark 4:35-41 recounts the story of when Jesus fell asleep while He and the disciples were traveling across the sea to reach the other side. He was woken up from His rest by the frantic cries of His disciples. Listen to what they said:

"Teacher, do you not care that we are about to die?" (Verse 38b AMP)

How many times have we questioned the Lord in similar fashion? This is one of those awkward honest moments when the preacher asks a question like this in the middle of his sermon and you aren't sure if you should blurt out your shortcomings for all to hear or simply hang your head in shame.

Listen, each of us is a work in progress. We have all had moments where we questioned the Lord's intentions in our life, questioned His love for us, questioned what He was up to, and dare I say, even blamed Him for things that He had no part in...

Be encouraged today!! God is so much bigger than any of our doubts! The key is this, don't stay there. The sooner we learn to cast down those doubts in favor of His Word, the better off we will be.

Aren't you glad that God wrote into the Bible so many shortcomings about men and women just like us?! They serve as shortcuts, so we don't have to make the same mistakes or at least dwell on them for nearly as long! They show us the alternative of listening, trusting, and obeying. They provide us the awesome gift of hindsight, which we can then turn into foresight and choose to trust in Jesus from the get-go!

Let's go back up to verse 35. Jesus said *"Let US go over to the other side..."*

Listen, God's Word is His will! Here's some good news:

"For all the promises of God in Him are Yes, and in Him Amen, to the glory of God through us."
~II Corinthians 1:20 (NKJV)

"So shall My word be that goes forth from My mouth; It shall not return to Me void, but it shall accomplish what I please, and it shall prosper in the thing for which I sent it."
~Isaiah 55:11 (NKJV)

The Lord doesn't throw words around flippantly. If He says it, it is so!

Jesus told them they were all going to the other side, so their response to the storm should have been, or could have been to rebuke it themselves on the authority of Jesus' Word! Something along these lines, "Storm, shut up! Jesus said we are all going to the other side, and that's exactly what we are going to do!"

I am being facetious, of course, and I love how Jesus simply and graciously said *"Peace, be still."*

I really want to encourage you today! Are you facing a storm? Are there things coming against you that are contrary to what you know God has for you? Don't be discouraged. Get God's Word on the matter and speak that Word to the storm in Jesus' name! Tell it to be still!

In our journey of getting to know Him more, it is imperative that we realize once and for all that He is for us, not against us! That He cares for you and me more than we could ever know!

We don't have to question His care for us anymore when the storms of life arise. We can use His Word to calm those storms because He has given us the authority to do so!

Be encouraged today and let this simple but amazing truth sink deep within your heart today:

Jesus loves me, this I know, for the Bible tells me so!

Challenge Corner

- Has there been a time in your life when you questioned God? Doubted Him? What was the final outcome of that instance? (For me, I have jumped to conclusions so many times or even done things and then thought, this is it, He is done with me... only to have Him chase me down once again!)

_____

_____

_____

_____

_____

_____

_____

_____

_____

_____

_____

_____

- We serve a God who is Just, yes! Holy, yes! Pure, Yes! But He is also long-suffering! Aren't you glad?! Write down a time or times when God could have dealt with you more harshly, but instead dealt with you like a loving Father...

_____

_____

_____

_____

_____

_____

_____

_____

_____

_____

_____

_____

_____

_____

_____

_____

_____

_____

_____

_____

_____

_____

_____

_____

"For God so loved the world that He gave His only begotten Son, that whoever believes in Him should not perish but have everlasting life."
~John 3:16 (NKJV)

- The more we grow in our walk with the Lord, the more we will come to realize our need for Him! This is truly a lifelong pursuit, but one that gets richer and deeper as time goes by if we continue to abide in Him and His Word! How long have you been born-again? Are you born-again? If it's been awhile, then how has your relationship with the Lord changed over the years? If it's been just a short while, what are some things you wish could be more full, more vibrant in your walk with Him?

_____

_____

_____

_____

_____

_____

_____

_____

_____

_____

_____

_____

_____

- What are some practical steps you can take, beginning today, to grow closer to the Lord? To get to know Him more?

_____

_____

_____

_____

_____

_____

_____

Mornings with Jesus ☼

"SEEK AND YOU SHALL FIND"

T	D	O	U	B	T	S	U	M	C	S	S	I	E	S	Y	A
Y	L	T	N	A	P	P	I	L	F	P	R	H	C	A	M	Z
L	E	M	S	E	V	O	L	S	U	S	E	J	O	C	F	Z
O	Q	Q	D	S	B	L	F	K	W	C	I	Q	P	I	F	J
V	S	U	Y	E	W	R	J	L	A	N	O	G	K	A	N	U
I	E	P	E	V	E	U	Z	B	Q	N	A	R	V	E	U	A
N	A	D	U	S	A	P	I	G	M	X	I	O	W	Q	Q	S
G	O	S	J	E	T	D	E	O	Z	I	R	X	A	E	D	L
K	F	T	U	U	E	I	Q	R	T	S	E	T	L	C	P	E
I	G	O	R	N	Q	S	O	G	E	H	H	R	K	W	D	E
N	A	R	K	I	Q	W	L	N	U	E	E	Q	X	E	I	P
D	L	M	P	T	C	U	C	Q	E	S	L	R	C	Y	O	P
N	I	S	G	N	Q	H	U	D	O	D	U	T	S	H	V	X
E	L	P	W	O	W	W	E	L	Y	C	N	B	T	I	X	P
S	E	T	K	C	C	G	C	R	L	E	V	T	B	E	D	D
S	E	I	J	B	I	N	T	E	N	T	I	O	N	S	M	E
G	N	I	R	E	F	F	U	S	G	N	O	L	D	N	E	Z

Mettle   Sea of Galilee   Favor

Asleep   Test   Storms

Doubts   Lovingkindness   Closer

Intentions   Other Side   Richer

Void   Questioned   Jesus Loves Me

Abide   Flippantly   Deeper

Long Suffering   Continue   Walk

"For the Son of Man is
come to seek and to
save that which was
lost."
(Luke 19:10)

I Know A Guy

By: Joshua Scott Zeitz

Carrying weights and pain?
Heavily disdained?
Like everything you do is stained?

You're not alone!
I know a guy,
I know His name!

No longer making gains?
Black clouds and rain?
Forget the silver lining,
all you feel is shame?

You're not alone!
I know a guy,
I spoke His name!

Head up? Eyes strained!
Perk up? Smile feigned!
Look up? Hope waned!

You're not alone!
I know a guy,
I've felt His flame!

Remember

"...that this may be a sign among you when your children ask in time to come, saying, 'What do these stones mean to you?' Then you shall answer them that the waters of the Jordan were cut off before the ark of the covenant of the LORD; when it crossed over the Jordan, the waters of the Jordan were cut off. And these stones shall be for a memorial to the children of Israel forever."

~Joshua 4:6-7 (NKJV)

Sometimes, we, as flawed human beings, have a hard time remembering the good things the Lord has done for us and through us!

We tend to have this negative bent to us that, more often than not, gets us stuck in ruts of stinkin thinkin.

However, the Lord doesn't want us living there! He wants us free!

Perhaps one of the best ways to be free from stinkin thinkin is to purposefully call to mind all the things the Lord has done for us and in us!

When we are focused on Him and His goodness, it's very hard to be negative, fearful, anxious, or whatever goes against the freedom that Jesus died to provide for us.

God has done more for you and me than we even realize!

If you are struggling right now to find something to be thankful for, you probably have a bad case of stinkin thinkin. But don't be discouraged, we are in this together, on this journey to know Him more!

Be encouraged today. He is for you, not against you! Today, I want to simply take some time and remember what He has done for us.

If you need a starting place, start here:

You deserved Hell, but God gave you Heaven!
He gave you what you didn't deserve, His grace! His forgiveness! His mercy!

I want to challenge you right now: Take out some paper and a pencil, your phone, your computer, whatever you can write or type on and make a remembrance list.

I want you to write down everything the Lord has done either for you, in you, or through you!

We serve an awesome God who doesn't simply want to give us stuff; He wants to do mighty works through us! He wants to cause us to be the answer to other people's prayers!

What Has He Done for You?

Write it down.

Each time you write something down; I want you, out loud, to thank Him!

When we build a habit of being thankful, of being grateful for the awesome God we serve, not only will it allow us to grow in our relationship with Him, but it will also make room for us to gain an eternal perspective, to see the things that truly matter!

This will in turn make us free to share the Good News with others. We won't be tied down by worry, fear, doubt, or stinkin thinkin!

When we look back on these lists, or when our children, family, or friends ask about these lists, we can tell them that *this* is when God delivered me! *This* is when God did this through me! *This* is when God provided for me! *This* is when I saw no way, but He made a way! *This* is when God healed me! *This* is when God saved me! *This* is when...

I have great news for you today: If He did it then, He can do it again!

I have more great news for you: Our lists, our memorials to His goodness cannot only be written down on paper, they can be worn on our faces, portrayed in our attitudes, sung from our hearts, and lived out in our lives!

Listen, we ARE living breathing testaments to God's Goodness!

The very fact that we are alive is a testimony to His grace!

The very fact that we aren't in Hell is a testament to His mercy!

The very fact that we have joy is a testament to the fact that He still saves, He still heals, and He still delivers!!!

We have so much more to be thankful for than we realize. On our journey to know Him more, know this: He is worthy of the highest praise! Give Him that today, won't you?!

Challenge Corner

*   Write down your remembrance list and keep it somewhere you can see it often and add to it often!

- Prayerfully consider who you would like to share this list with - a close friend, a family member, a spouse? This could be an awesome transition into talking about the Lord with someone!

_____
_____
_____
_____
_____
_____
_____
_____
_____
_____
_____
_____
_____
_____
_____
_____
_____
_____
_____
_____
_____
_____
_____
_____
_____
_____
_____

➡ When was the last time you stopped what you were doing and just gave the Lord the praise He is so deserving of?

How about right now?!

Mornings with Jesus

"SEEK AND YOU SHALL FIND"

A	F	N	J	C	V	L	Q	P	B	H	R	X	G	K	D	J
E	A	D	S	C	P	H	B	K	R	E	X	M	C	V	E	D
F	M	E	J	U	E	E	V	I	G	R	O	F	R	M	Y	O
A	I	V	A	A	E	S	I	A	R	P	L	F	F	I	A	T
Z	L	T	L	Y	J	O	U	R	N	E	Y	T	F	N	R	N
U	Y	S	N	E	R	D	L	I	H	C	S	H	K	D	T	E
R	E	M	E	M	B	E	R	D	F	L	A	A	H	U	R	M
D	E	L	I	V	E	R	S	V	P	W	T	N	E	F	O	A
I	I	U	M	W	D	H	D	P	V	S	J	K	J	C	P	T
H	W	Y	C	R	E	M	J	C	E	Q	T	F	Y	C	U	S
S	S	S	X	U	E	C	A	H	V	Y	E	U	Q	V	C	E
A	W	L	M	X	U	X	G	R	E	Z	I	L	A	E	R	T
V	C	L	O	U	W	I	D	E	S	E	R	V	E	D	I	S
E	K	K	L	T	H	Z	D	G	C	O	Q	C	P	C	Z	F
S	C	T	W	E	E	S	G	F	F	R	I	E	N	D	S	A
Y	P	T	Y	B	H	T	R	A	N	S	I	T	I	O	N	L
R	D	Y	A	L	L	S	P	F	L	A	W	E	D	C	Z	B

Flawed	Thankful	Mercy
Realize	Praise	Heals
Remember	Mind	Journey
Forgive	Friends	Children
Highest	Testament	Deserved
Hell	Portrayed	Delivers
Family	Saves	Transition

"For I know the thoughts that I think toward you, saith the LORD, thoughts of peace, and not of evil, to give you an expected end."
(Jeremiah 29:11)

Timmy Falls Down
(A Poem About Getting Back Up!)
By: Joshua Scott Zeitz

Timmy the frog was an excellent hopper,
The pride of the team,
A real show stopper!
He sprinted so fast,
they called him the motor
nary a hurdle,
He couldn't leap over!
He tore down the track
with the greatest of ease
Easy to miss,
should you blink from a sneeze!
The top of the podium,
week after week.
Til one day poor Timmy
went weak on his feet
first a split then a splink
then a sploosh then a splat
Til Timmy stopped skidding
lying flat on his back!
First an "Ooo," then an "Ahh!"
Then a "Yikes," then an "Ouch!"

Poor Timmy lay wheezing
For his wind was knocked out!
Ahead of the game
At the blow of the whistle
He took up the rear
they blew by like a missile
Nary a runner
stopped to pay heed
And nigh did the doctor,
there wasn't a need!
For just as the last frog
gave him a pass,
Timmy stood up
to join back the pack!
With a flick and a kick,
and a flack and a flutter,
Timmy gave chase
with nary a stutter!
It happened so quick,
Nigh a word could they mutter!
Forlorn from falling,
He could have cried, "Fold!"
Instead he roared, "ALL IN!"
and took home the gold!

Think Bigger of Him

"Therefore, let us [with privilege] *approach the throne of grace* [that is, the throne of God's gracious favor] *with confidence and without fear, so that we may receive mercy* [for our failures] *and find* [His amazing] *grace to help in time of need* [an appropriate blessing, coming just at the right moment]."
~Hebrews 4:16 (AMP)

How many times have we gone to God with half prayers, never truly believing He will answer us to the fullest? We go to Him with outstretched hands begging for something, anything that He can spare.

"God, if you could just help me pay this one bill, pay half the rent, or buy this old vehicle; please Lord, anything you can spare. I know I don't deserve it..."

Hearing it like that may sound a bit over the top, but it's so true. Many times, we find ourselves pleading and begging God for help instead of boldly believing that He is able to do exceedingly abundantly above all we could ask, think, or even imagine!

I love how the Amplified Bible words it:

"Now to Him who is able to [carry out His purpose and] *do superabundantly more than all that we dare ask or think* [infinitely beyond our greatest prayers, hopes, or dreams], *according to His power that is at work within us,"*
~Ephesians 3:20 (AMP)

Be encouraged today! He doesn't want to help you with only one bill, He wants to provide for all your needs according to His riches in glory by Christ Jesus! He wants you to have the best!

He is your Heavenly Father, and He loves you - more than you could ever dream or imagine. You are ever before Him, in His mind. The Bible says if you were to try to count God's precious thoughts towards you, they are innumerable like the sand on the seashore! (See Psalm 139)

The Bible says, if your son asks you for bread, will you give him a stone? It goes on later to say, so then you, who possess an evil nature, know how to give good gifts to your children, therefore HOW MUCH MORE will He give good things to those who ask Him! (See Matthew 7:7-11)

Today, as you go before your Heavenly Father, come boldly before His throne and believe that he is able and willing to do far above all you could ever imagine in your life! He wants to!

Think Bigger of Him!

Challenge Corner

- Have you ever gone to God with begging prayers? If so, you are not alone.

_____

_____

_____

_____

- Read Psalm 139. How does God view you?

_____

_____

_____

_____

_____

_____

_____

_____

_____

_____

_____

- The Bible says we must believe that He is and that He is a rewarder of them that diligently seek Him. Do you believe this? How can we diligently seek Him?

_____

_____

_____

_____

_____

_____

_____

_____

_____

_____

_____

_____

- Why do you think God wants to bless us? To provide for us? (Hint: We freely receive so that we can freely give! We love, because He first loved us!)

_____

_____

_____

_____

_____

_____

_____

_____

_____

_____

_____

_____

_____

Mornings with Jesus

"SEEK AND YOU SHALL FIND"

R	E	C	E	I	V	E	L	X	E	S	P	L	D	R	U	U
U	V	W	F	M	H	A	Y	C	N	F	E	G	S	L	B	Z
O	E	N	O	R	H	T	N	N	Y	N	Y	A	O	X	E	R
E	E	V	I	G	Q	E	P	L	I	L	N	V	L	J	G	E
T	V	U	L	T	D	E	E	G	O	D	E	J	A	L	G	D
H	S	O	E	I	B	E	A	S	Y	K	B	J	A	E	I	R
Z	S	E	F	P	R	M	E	R	C	L	E	W	J	T	N	A
S	H	N	L	F	I	A	M	B	I	J	D	K	A	C	G	W
U	O	T	D	L	S	L	P	N	T	Z	K	L	K	M	N	E
C	W	U	Q	H	U	K	M	T	U	E	R	K	O	H	X	R
U	U	R	O	S	Z	F	F	G	V	Q	K	Y	N	B	P	H
B	S	R	N	A	B	U	N	D	A	N	T	L	Y	I	D	B
X	E	D	T	L	E	V	E	I	L	E	B	X	G	W	H	M
W	E	R	W	Q	Q	D	I	L	I	G	E	N	T	L	Y	T
W	K	K	N	E	R	O	M	H	C	U	M	W	O	H	V	I
Q	X	U	U	O	U	T	S	T	R	E	T	C	H	E	D	U
I	N	N	U	M	E	R	A	B	L	E	E	P	V	D	X	F

Believe	Receive	Sand
Fullest	Love	How Much More
Rewarder	Diligently	Imagine
Throne	Seek	Seashore
Boldly	Innumerable	Confidence
Freely	Abundantly	Think
Give	Outstretched	Begging

"One thing have I desired of the LORD, that will I seek after: That I may dwell in the house of the LORD all the days of my life, To behold the beauty of the LORD, and to enquire in his temple."
(Psalm 27:4)

A Million Reasons
By: Joshua Scott Zeitz

I'm done trying to fit in
living for the weekend
throwing up these prayers
for the things that im weak in
wondering if the Lord
even hears what im speaking
wondering if I'm real
if I'm living what im preaching
dreading these church plays
hoping I'll just sleep in
a slave to the script
to the lies that I'm steeped in
drowning in my sorrow
and this ain't even the deep end
knee deep in the muck
a wolf shedding off my sheep skin

lock the doors bar the gates
don't want to let the thief in
got this truck on my chest
pressures got me heavy breathing
pass the buck, pass the puff
surely God knows I've been cheating
layin up
fronting tough
surely God knows I'm a weakling
exercising that's what's up
gotta get rid of these demons
selfish pride self aside
salt and light is my new season
sing it out sing it loud
got like a million reasons!

Thank-filled

"It is good to give thanks to the LORD, And to sing praises to Your name, O Most High; To declare Your loving kindness in the morning, And Your faithfulness every night," ~Psalms 92:1-2 (NKJV)

The news report for today: We live in a messed-up world, and right now we are living in some crazy times.

Can I encourage you for a moment?! The Bible says there's nothing new under the sun. It takes very little courage or gusto to be conformed to this world, to be a bearer of bad news.

However, you want to know what takes much courage, especially in the face of our culture?

Thankfulness!

Being thankful, being someone who makes a habit out of praising the Lord regardless of what is going on, in spite of what the news reports say, in spite of what the bank account says, in spite of what the doctor reports, this takes courage, and it's in this place where you will receive your healing, your victory, and your peace!

It's in this place where you will be ready to share the gospel with someone!

The world is full of people declaring bad news, but we have a higher calling. If you are a born-again believer, you have been commissioned to declare the Good News! You've been called by the King of kings and Lord of lords to declare boldly and bravely another Way: His name is Jesus!

You want to know the best way to keep your spiritual tank filled? Be thank-filled!

Thankfulness is the key to bringing the power of God in your life like no other!

When we make a habit of praising the Lord regardless of what is going on around us, or in us, we are positioned to receive and give what others cannot!

While the rest of the world is focused on the latest craze, we can be focused on Jesus! While the rest of the disciples are shaking in their boots in the boat thinking they just saw a ghost, we can be out walking on the waves with Jesus!

Even if everyone around you is talking about fear, bad news, the latest political drama, or whatever, you can take a stand today.

"I will bless the Lord at all times; His praise shall continually be in my mouth!" ~Psalm 34:1 (NKJV)

Learn to live with courage. Learn to live with an attitude of gratitude. The Lord has done so much for you! Take some time today to give Him thanks - to be thank-filled. Do this and there won't be room for anything else!

Challenge Corner

- Do you struggle with being drawn to negativity? Do you love to hear the latest crazy thing going on in the world? The latest juicy piece of gossip at the office or in the church? If so, be encouraged! The Good News is this: You can turn it around today!

_____

_____

_____

_____

_____

_____

_____

_____

_____

_____

- What are some practical steps we can take to begin blessing the Lord at all times?

_____

_____

_____

_____

_____

_____

_____

_____

_____

_____

_____

_____

_____

_____

_____

_____

_____

_____

_____

The Bible says be thankful IN everything, not FOR everything. Therefore we don't have to be hooky spooky and go about thanking God for every single thing that happens or comes our way. It's not a sin to get frustrated when you're stuck in traffic, you're standing in a long line, or if someone says or does something mean to us. However, in spite of these things, we can build a habit of praising God anyway! By doing this, we will not only take the power back to our emotions, but also position ourselves to be ministers to others. Listen, when we are focused on the pain, it's hard to think about others. But when we praise the Lord, not for the pain, but in spite of the pain, we will sail above the mess and be able to see from His perspective. In essence, we will be able to see others who don't have the same hope and peace we do, and be able to offer it to them!

Mornings with Jesus

"SEEK AND YOU SHALL FIND"

B	N	T	H	G	Y	E	K	Y	S	Q	C	X	D	W	Q	B
E	D	U	T	I	T	A	R	G	L	S	P	O	O	K	Y	E
R	B	J	O	Y	C	P	E	M	B	A	D	N	E	W	S	D
E	P	S	C	X	D	H	Q	G	E	X	Q	Y	P	G	O	U
H	R	W	X	O	D	E	C	L	A	R	E	F	P	D	G	T
G	A	E	C	W	M	D	L	I	L	R	H	R	X	F	O	I
I	I	N	A	J	K	M	B	L	I	K	U	N	S	R	S	T
H	S	D	L	B	U	E	I	P	I	P	M	O	Q	B	S	T
B	E	O	L	B	S	N	R	S	O	F	T	Z	C	K	I	A
M	S	O	I	H	E	F	F	M	S	V	K	I	Y	P	P	R
X	G	G	N	D	P	F	K	W	P	I	N	N	B	C	B	Z
N	K	N	G	H	G	U	S	T	O	K	O	F	A	A	Y	K
O	V	L	Q	E	C	N	E	S	S	E	E	N	V	H	H	C
E	L	I	M	A	R	T	X	E	J	N	C	L	E	O	T	Z
F	E	P	O	H	A	X	P	J	X	L	A	V	I	D	Q	C
B	W	J	M	U	T	S	Y	B	P	Z	E	F	D	C	V	N
T	D	A	J	D	L	E	P	S	O	G	P	Y	C	V	Z	P

Thank Filled	Peace	Gratitude
Praises	Hope	Spooky
Extra Mile	Commissioned	Essence
Courage	Declare	Gossip
Gusto	Bad News	Higher
Habit	Good News	Calling
Gospel	Attitude	Key

"And thou, Solomon my son: if thou seek him, he will be found of thee; but if thou forsake him, he will cast thee off forever."
(1 Chronicles 28:9b)

More Than You Know - Part 1

"Who comforts and encourages us in every trouble so that we will be able to comfort and encourage those who are in any kind of trouble, with the comfort with which we ourselves are comforted by God." ~II Corinthians 1:4 (AMP)

I love the Lord!

He has this awesome ability to cut right to the heart of a matter in a way that leaves me without excuse, but also provides plenty of room for mercy! The way He handles me no matter how foolish, selfish, or childish I've been, makes me want to tell others, "Come meet this awesome Jesus who found me right where I was and offered me forgiveness, life, hope, and peace!"

Listen, you are so valuable to God! More than you know!

John Chapter 4 tells of the interaction between the Samaritan woman and Jesus at the well, and before their conversation ended, Jesus managed to cut right to the woman's heart revealing that He knew of her previous and current troubles with men, He knew her sin, and yet He offered her eternal life right where she was!

At that moment, when Jesus revealed these things to her, she could have gotten offended and walked away. She could have received her forgiveness from Him, but then never told anyone. She could have run back to the village and claimed all manner of evil against Him. There could have been a much different result. But instead she went back to her people and declared to them boldly, *"Come meet a man that told me everything I've ever done!"*

When Jesus truly gets a hold of your life, He heals you from the inside out! He takes away the shame and guilt attached to the sins and mistakes you've committed. He heals you in a way that you are free to declare:

"Come meet a man that told me everything I've ever done!"

Be encouraged today, you have so much more to offer than you know!

What has the Lord done in your life? What obstacles, sins, addictions, and weights has He freed you from?

What victories, healings, miracles, comforts, and encouragements has He offered you?

I want to challenge you today. Don't run from those things. Look and pray for opportunities to share them with others!

We live in a society that values putting your best foot forward, putting up facades, and being flawless. But can I encourage you today? Without Him (Jesus), we can do nothing!

It's in this place of vulnerability and humility that we can be a witness to the people around us!

So many people are hurting, feel lost, and are doing the same thing as everyone else: pretending to be okay. We have the chance to offer them the same hope that God has so feely offered us!

Don't hide what God has done for you, in you, and through you - share it! You have more to offer than you know!

The Samaritan woman did just that, *"Now many Samaritans from that city believed in Him and trusted Him [as Savior] because of what the woman said when she testified, "He told me all the things that I have done.""* ~John 4:39 (AMP)

Take a moment and reflect on all that God has done for you - more than you know!

God is bigger than any problem you have
or will ever encounter!

Challenge Corner

- Does the idea of sharing what the Lord has done in your life frighten you? If so, why? If not, when was the last time you did so?

_____

_____

_____

_____

_____

_____

_____

_____

- What has the Lord done in your life? What kinds of things has he delivered you from? Healed you from? Write them down and prayerfully consider to whom and when to share them!

_____

_____

_____

_____

_____

_____

_____

_____

_____

_____

_____

_____

_____

_____

- You have more to offer than you know! Why? Because He has provided more than we realize! What kinds of things do we have to offer others because of what Jesus has done for us and in us?

_____
_____
_____
_____
_____
_____
_____
_____
_____
_____
_____
_____
_____
_____
_____
_____
_____
_____
_____
_____
_____
_____
_____
_____

Your story is God's story, share it!

The Gospel's Plea
By: Joshua Scott Zeitz

Eternity is calling
Don't let it slip away
This life won't last forever
No time to play it safe
I know you've heard Him calling
So this could be your day
I know that you've been hiding
Looking to run away
He knows it all already
Just surrender to His grace
He longs to call you child
Just surrender to the chase
I know you think He's angry
And long ago He was
But Jesus paid the price for sin
He shed His precious blood
Three days and nights
The earth was shook
But then he rose again!
And all for joy that laid before,
The chance to call you friend!

Mornings with Jesus

"SEEK AND YOU SHALL FIND"

F	R	Y	O	D	Z	H	F	C	B	Z	P	B	D	D	D	W
R	F	L	G	X	Q	A	R	D	R	V	Y	C	E	L	O	S
C	G	F	U	D	C	V	E	H	E	D	P	H	C	R	O	U
M	Y	W	K	A	H	R	U	L	G	C	E	I	L	O	P	W
O	A	D	D	Z	E	T	B	M	B	B	O	E	A	W	P	G
R	P	E	O	F	N	A	W	M	Z	L	P	P	R	H	O	F
E	S	V	F	E	R	T	R	A	E	H	L	V	E	E	R	Y
L	F	O	M	E	W	S	K	T	K	N	E	J	N	I	T	T
W	K	O	N	S	P	F	S	T	R	O	F	M	O	C	U	I
N	M	L	O	C	T	E	T	E	Z	O	R	O	K	U	N	L
M	U	G	C	B	Y	K	Y	R	Y	W	R	D	K	P	I	I
V	B	E	L	B	A	U	L	A	V	T	O	R	Q	X	T	M
S	E	G	A	R	U	O	C	N	E	T	E	E	E	J	I	U
G	E	G	N	E	L	L	A	H	C	B	T	I	C	B	E	H
T	E	S	T	I	F	I	E	D	R	K	L	R	C	F	S	D
Z	Q	A	D	L	G	E	D	I	S	N	I	X	Z	O	T	T
O	V	I	C	T	O	R	I	E	S	S	H	A	R	E	S	K

More	Heart	People
Valuable	Vulnerable	Challenge
Comforts	Humility	Inside
Matter	Encourages	Offered
Opportunities	Moment	Declare
Facades	Testified	Victories
Share	Society	World

"I would seek unto God, And unto God would I commit my cause Which doeth great things and unsearchable; Marvellous things without number"
(Job 5:8,9)

Rested

"Peace I leave with you; My [perfect] *peace I give to you; not as the world gives do I give to you. Do not let your heart be troubled, nor let it be afraid.* [Let My perfect peace calm you in every circumstance and give you courage and strength for every challenge.]*"* ~John 14:27 (AMP)

Ever feel tired or sluggish during the day, like you just need a little extra sleep? I know I do! If I am short one hour of sleep for whatever reason, it messes with my entire day.

Likewise, failing to spend one-on-one time with the Lord is a recipe for disaster. Jesus is called the Prince of Peace (see Isaiah 9:6), the Bishop of our Souls (see 1 Peter 2:25), and the Author and Finisher of our faith (see Hebrews 12:2).

When our minds and hearts are stayed on Him, we feel rested, and ultimately, we are available to be used by God to bless others.

The awesomely Good News is this: we are never alone! When Jesus ascended into Heaven, He did a tag-team hand off with the Holy Spirit who has come to reside within every born-again believer!

This means that we have 24/7 access to the throne of Grace!

What a mighty God we serve!

Listen, we live in a world that wants to chew us up and spit us out. But take heart because Jesus has overcome the world! (See John 16:33) He said, I leave my Peace, not as the world, with some twisted, ulterior motive, but as I give, to bring you hope, life, and joy!

John 10:10 says it's the thief who wants to steal, kill, and destroy you, but Jesus wants to bring you life and it more abundantly!

Therefore, take heart today. Run to Jesus! He wants to make you free and fill you up so much that you always feel rested in Him. It's in this place of rest that you are ready and willing to reach out to those around you!

This world has nothing on you when you are resting in Him!

***Having trouble entering that rest? Start here: do the 5, 5, 5 (credit to Pastor Jim Frease):

5 minutes of Bible, 5 minutes Praise, 5 minutes of Prayer.

Don't be discouraged! You got this! Start right where you are and do this simple thing. It may be awkward at first, but if you do this on a consistent basis, over time, you will find that your time in these things will increase and your walk with the Lord will grow by leaps and bounds. You will become rested!

Challenge Corner

- At this moment in your life, do you feel rested in the Lord? Completely rested? Rested enough that you are able and willing to share what the Lord has done in your life with others? Rested enough to not be bothered by the ups and downs in the economy? Rested enough to not be stressed by the duties of everyday life?

_____

_____

_____

_____

_____

_____

_____

_____

_____

_____

_____

_____

_____

- Wherever you are right now, in whatever season of life you are in, be encouraged! Jesus wants to give you rest! Cast your cares upon Him today, He cares for you immensely, more than you know. And He has promised to never leave you nor forsake you!

- Make a list today of all the things that you are thankful for:

_____

_____

_____

_____

_____

_____

_____

_____

_____

_____

_____

_____

_____

_____

_____

_____

_____

_____

_____

_____

_____

_____

_____

"Come to Me, all you who labor and are heavy laden, and I will give you rest."
~Matthew 11:28 (NKJV)

Mornings with Jesus

"SEEK AND YOU SHALL FIND"

O	F	M	F	V	C	R	B	R	X	E	R	D	M	B	G	R
V	I	J	L	O	J	I	Z	U	C	V	E	D	B	O	Z	O
J	N	H	Z	Z	S	V	Q	N	Z	I	C	E	W	U	Y	I
P	I	P	R	H	R	O	H	E	B	T	I	T	H	N	F	R
E	S	L	O	Q	G	H	D	V	G	O	P	S	Z	D	V	E
R	H	P	B	Z	U	T	B	A	T	M	E	E	P	S	Y	T
F	E	H	X	T	M	E	E	E	G	V	H	R	A	A	S	L
E	R	S	B	N	F	X	O	H	D	V	E	N	C	B	E	U
C	R	I	T	E	A	S	C	E	N	D	E	D	O	J	L	L
T	O	G	C	M	V	R	G	B	A	D	U	E	N	R	E	C
M	H	G	O	O	E	D	I	S	E	R	S	P	S	W	V	T
A	T	U	U	M	U	C	D	W	B	A	E	J	I	E	P	O
E	U	L	R	G	X	J	K	S	E	A	F	V	S	H	R	I
T	A	S	A	K	M	C	U	R	C	X	D	F	T	S	N	J
G	N	Y	G	I	B	V	C	E	J	T	A	Q	E	A	J	F
A	V	H	E	L	I	N	R	P	S	T	R	E	N	G	T	H
T	L	O	W	X	I	L	O	L	G	S	H	F	T	S	V	R

Peace	Rested	Bishop
Sluggish	Perfect	Ascended
Author	Finisher	Consistent
Motive	Ulterior	Leaps
Recipe	Courage	Increase
Strength	Reside	Moment
Heaven	Tag Team	Bounds

"Who will have all men to be saved, and to come unto the knowledge of the truth."
(1 Timothy 2:4)

Smooth Things Over

"Create in me a clean heart, O God, and renew a right and steadfast spirit within me. Restore to me the joy of Your salvation and sustain me with a willing spirit. Then I will teach transgressors Your ways, and sinners shall be converted and return to You." ~Psalms 51:10, 12-13 (AMP)

One of our favorite family pastimes is watching food competitions on television. After watching several of these shows, there's something strangely wonderful that I have noticed. It's easy to sit on my side of things and critique the people doing all the work!

"Hey, do this or do that! Why are you doing that?!" We scream at the T.V. in a matter-of-fact way, as if they can hear us, or better yet, as if we could really do any better if placed in their position.

It's easy to do this very thing in our Christian walk as well. If we aren't mindful, it can become quite easy to begin pointing the finger at everyone around us, telling them what to do, what to believe, how to believe, and critiquing them on their faith or lack thereof.

For me personally, this is something I struggled with early on in my walk with the Lord. Simply put, I was rough around the edges! This caused me to have a very critical spirit, which meant that rather than being able to share the gospel with people, I was more focused on their supposed or assumed lack of spirituality.

Listen, Jesus didn't say go into the entire world and tell people how bad they are, or go and tell them how lacking their faith is, He said share the gospel!

The best way I've found to do this is by spending time with the Lord! Only when I take the time to reflect on my own walk with Him, allowing Him to mold me and make me, am I able to be a viable witness for Him and His Kingdom.

The more time I spend with Jesus, the more like Him I become! The more time I spend in His presence the more like Him I speak and do.

We all have rough edges that need to be smoothed over. Be encouraged today! The Bible is the best refining and smoothing tool there is. Allow it to smooth things over in your own life and watch how much easier it becomes to share the Good News with others!

Feeling a bit rough today? Don't be discouraged; spend a little extra time in His presence! Praise Him. Put some worship music on. Allow the Bible to pour over you. Pray like David did, *"Create in me a clean heart..."* (See Psalm 51)

What a difference it makes when, rather than telling people how bad they are, we start showing them how good God is!

Smooth things over today in your own walk, and then get out there and share the Good News!

Challenge Corner

- What are some rough edges that need to be smoothed in your life? (Don't see any rough edges? Perhaps you could stand to spend some more time in the Word.) Just remember, whatever God reveals, He wants to heal. So don't be afraid to go through the process with Him.

_____

_____

_____

_____

_____

_____

_____

_____

_____

_____

- Do you enjoy talking with others about the Lord? If not, what are some practical steps you can take to build this desire?

_____

_____

_____

_____

_____

_____

_____

_____

- David was called a man after God's own heart by God Himself. What an awesome compliment! We can be like David in this manner. What are some things we can do to begin sharing this trait as well? To love the things God loves, and hate the things He hates? Listen, we all make mistakes. We all blow it from time to time. It's not the fact that we fail that keeps us from being a person after His heart, it's the unwillingness to repent, to get back up, to run into His arms. Therefore whatever you are facing today, I encourage you to run *to* Him, not from Him, and allow Him to smooth things over!

_____

_____

_____

_____

_____

_____

_____

_____

_____

_____

_____

Mornings with Jesus ☼

"SEEK AND YOU SHALL FIND"

Z	L	A	D	O	F	U	K	I	N	G	D	O	M	D	D	B
M	R	B	P	S	T	E	A	D	F	A	S	T	C	A	N	A
T	F	F	K	N	H	T	O	O	M	S	F	W	T	T	B	R
L	H	O	D	T	N	E	M	I	L	P	M	O	C	E	B	E
C	O	M	P	E	T	I	T	I	O	N	S	A	V	L	L	S
N	O	I	T	I	S	O	P	N	Y	W	F	E	P	E	N	T
D	U	Z	S	O	R	N	F	R	K	U	N	T	T	V	V	O
L	P	X	V	H	U	O	D	J	W	O	Y	I	J	I	K	R
R	S	G	E	O	V	I	A	B	L	E	C	R	O	S	Q	E
C	R	E	A	T	E	T	U	D	S	C	P	O	Y	I	O	M
W	E	H	B	W	E	A	T	W	C	U	P	V	H	O	F	K
O	N	V	Q	D	D	V	O	L	L	L	H	A	D	N	G	F
R	I	A	H	W	G	L	L	A	D	G	E	F	I	D	T	H
S	F	Q	C	J	E	A	Z	J	U	I	A	A	S	H	P	T
H	E	A	U	J	S	S	C	O	M	V	J	Y	N	Z	B	I
I	R	J	R	P	V	K	R	G	O	S	P	E	L	N	F	A
P	K	Q	G	N	I	U	Q	I	T	I	R	C	V	Q	N	F

Competitions	Restore	Edges
Smooth	Position	Compliment
Steadfast	Clean	Salvation
Critiquing	Gospel	Viable
Create	Kingdom	Worship
Faith	Favorite	Refiners
Television	Rough	Joy

"Jesus saith unto him, I am the way, the truth, and the life: no man cometh unto the Father, but by me."
(John 14:6)

Teddy and Shirley
(A Poem About Forgiveness)
By: Joshua Scott Zeitz

Teddy was an odd and curious fellow
with a slightly round paunch
that shook like green jello
he loved to eat berries,
and practice his cello
but more than that even
he loved to stay mellow
he wasn't at all the competitive sort
he didn't run fast, hop, or play sports
instead he loved thinking, writing, and reading
he really loved gardens
and didn't mind weeding
One day Teddy was out on the lawn
nose pressed to a book,
he gave a big yawn
slunk in his hammock
he drifted and nodded
while Shirley the Squirrel
stood near him and plotted
a devious grin
on her face did appear
while under her breath

she taunted and jeered
Shirley the Squirrel
was wiley and cunning
she snatched up the sheers
her plan simple, but stunning
the hammock gave way
as Shirley went running
First a snip, then a snap
Then a spill, then a splat
Teddy lay wheezing
flat on his back
She watched and she waited
from the tree she sat hiding
Waiting for Teddy to rant and start chiding
What she didn't expect
Came next in that moment
A friendship was born
From a choosing quite potent
"I forgive you dear Shirley!"
The words he did utter
His choice to forgive
Set her heart all aflutter
With a twinge and twang,
His forgiveness did cut her.
"I'm sorry dear Teddy!"
The only words she could mutter.

More Than A Feeling

"God is a Spirit: and they that worship him must worship him in spirit and in truth." ~John 4:24 (KJV)

Let's be honest for a moment, we don't always feel like doing certain things. I know I don't!

In like manner, I don't always feel God. In fact, I would say more often than not, I don't.

However, He has promised in His Word to never leave me or forsake me, so which am I to believe: My feelings or the Word?

This may seem like a clear-cut answer and perhaps, looking at it in hindsight, it is. But how many times when faced with various trials or circumstances do we think, "Where is God in all this?"

Short answer: Where He has always been!

Listen, God's Word is His will and His Word always supersedes our feelings and experiences.

You may say, "Yeah but I experienced this or that and it was contrary to the Word or this happened, and it didn't line up with the Bible..."

God's Word is forever settled in Heaven! (See Psalm 119:89)

Jesus is the same yesterday, today, and forever! (See Hebrews 13:8)

Be encouraged today: the sooner we get it settled in our hearts that God is not our *problem*, He is our *answer* and that the Word of God is our refuge and fortress, the better off we will be.

The key: Keep putting the Word in no matter what! Don't stop. Don't quit. Keep on keeping on!

If we do this, we will be like David in Psalm 34:1, *"I will bless the Lord at all times: his praise shall continually be in my mouth."*

The very things that used to bother us will seem like nothing anymore. The crazy things going on around us won't faze us. We will have a peace that passes understanding! It's in this place of total surrender to the Word that people will look at us and say things like, "I know this or that has happened to you or around you, so how can you have such peace?"

Bam! That's our door of opportunity to share the gospel!

No matter what things are looming overhead, we can hide under the wings of our Heavenly Father! This blessed assurance comes not from feelings, but from the Word of God, the Spirit of God!

"Let the peace of Christ
[the inner calm of one who walks daily with Him]

be the controlling factor in your hearts
[deciding and settling questions that arise].

To this peace indeed you were called as members in one body
[of believers].

And be thankful
[to God always]."

~Colossians 3:15 (AMP)

Jesus is not an experience, a trend, or a goose-bump. He is God, to be worshiped, praised, revered, and followed!

Challenge Corner

- Feelings are something we hear much about - they are in our movies, songs, books, and everyday lives. From an early age, we are bombarded with advertisements and all sorts of things telling us to live by and trust our feelings (follow our hearts). The problem with this is the Bible says the heart of man is desperately wicked. What does this mean in everyday life? It means that our feelings can't be trusted. Feelings are fickle. They are up one moment and down the next. Therefore to be led by our feelings equates to a life that is constantly up and down as well. How do we remedy this? By trusting in something more secure, namely, the Word of God! What are some practical steps we can begin taking today to follow after the Word rather than our feelings? To allow the Word to direct us and be our compass instead of our feelings?

- Have you ever spoken out of turn? Said something you later regretted? Done something you later regretted? More than likely, at that moment, you were in your feelings (motivated by them and whatever it was that made you say or do the thing that you later regretted), and that seemed like the only way. But after your feelings subsided, you realized that there was another, better, route to take! This is how it is to be led by feelings, to follow our hearts. Listen, following the Lord and His Word is always the best action! It may mean we have to wait or have to deny our flesh certain things, but the payoff is always worth the sacrifice!

- List some things that you have been thinking about recently. Perhaps there is a big decision coming up in your life? Or maybe there have just been some things that have been on your mind lately? Some choices to be made? How can you let the Word lead you in these things rather than your feelings? (Hint: Read Proverbs 3:5-6)

_____

_____

_____

_____

_____

_____

_____

_____

_____

_____

_____

_____

_____

_____

_____

_____

_____

_____

_____

_____

_____

_____

_____

_____

_____

_____

Mornings with Jesus

"SEEK AND YOU SHALL FIND"

C	D	E	H	I	N	D	S	I	G	H	T	G	T	W	P	C
E	P	I	S	W	L	X	T	C	H	O	I	C	E	S	G	T
C	H	M	S	J	R	M	W	N	U	W	Q	J	V	G	N	Q
I	V	J	E	T	E	P	M	G	E	Y	R	E	S	N	I	H
F	J	U	R	A	F	G	I	Z	L	M	A	F	O	I	M	Y
I	F	H	T	E	U	T	P	E	Y	G	O	K	D	L	O	M
R	O	E	R	Q	G	V	T	L	U	J	P	M	X	E	O	M
C	R	A	O	W	E	A	N	C	C	F	H	F	M	E	L	Y
A	E	R	F	R	R	I	G	O	V	V	K	U	W	F	M	B
S	V	T	U	E	S	E	C	N	E	I	R	E	P	X	E	V
I	E	S	P	C	C	E	F	S	E	T	T	L	E	D	N	X
W	R	S	O	L	L	I	W	O	R	S	H	I	P	J	V	C
N	E	C	M	T	C	X	O	R	O	T	C	A	F	C	A	O
D	C	X	Y	K	T	S	E	N	O	H	V	Z	A	A	M	D
V	S	A	L	S	U	P	E	R	S	E	D	E	S	E	A	Z
A	T	E	C	A	E	P	D	E	T	T	E	R	G	E	R	H
Q	J	G	X	P	R	O	M	I	S	E	D	W	S	S	I	I

Honest	Settled	Worship
Supersedes	Refuge	Hindsight
Feelings	Factor	Promised
Experiences	Hearts	Regretted
Forever	Peace	Choices
Fortress	Fickle	Moment
Looming	Sacrifice	Desperately

"For God so loved the world, that he gave his only begotten Son, that whosoever believeth in him should not perish, but have everlasting life."
(John 3:16)

Slow Down

"God is our refuge and strength,
A very present help in trouble."

"Be still and know that I am God;
I will be exalted among the nations;
I will be exalted in the earth!"

~Psalms 46:1, 10 (NKJV)

By show of hands, wherever you are reading this, how many of you have ever rushed into something too fast? Said something you regretted later? Did something you wished you hadn't?

Oh my! Both my hands and my feet are up!

Today, I just want to take a moment to be still before an awesome and mighty God! To acknowledge how good and faithful He is!

Be encouraged today, He is for you, not against you, and He cares about every facet of your life!

Yet how many times do we keep Him at bay until we feel we actually need Him? It looks something like this, "Okay God, I can handle all the smaller things like this, this, and this and I will call on you if/when this, this, or this arises."

In doing so, we try to compartmentalize Him, control Him, and treat Him, in essence, like a spare tire or a genie in a bottle.

Listen, I'm not saying we need to get all hooky spooky, "Oh Lord which flavor of gum do you wantest me to havest todayest...?" Yet, I am saying this: If we will purposefully practice putting Him first in our decision-making, our spending, our giving, our child-rearing, our work, if we will purposefully begin to allow Him to be involved in more areas of our life, we will find that the "small" things we used to keep Him out of, won't stress us out near as much.

Take some time today to think about some areas in your life that perhaps you have been trying to do on your own, without truly involving Him, and begin to seek scriptures for those areas. Talk to the Lord about them. Watch and see those areas begin to turn around for the better!

He will be exalted in the Earth! Allow Him to be exalted in your life today! Be still and know that He is God!

Is there a rap, poem, or prayer on your heart today?

_____

_____

_____

_____

_____

_____

_____

_____

_____

_____

_____

_____

_____

_____

_____

_____

_____

_____

_____

_____

_____

_____

_____

_____

_____

_____

_____

The Chicken Dream!

(A funny story about the necessity of seeking God!)

Recently, I had one of the craziest dreams!

In this dream, I was helping a lady shop. She took me through the aisles to look for some chicken. She had a small gathering approaching and needed something that would feed everyone.

After asking me a series of questions about three different types of chicken, she said, "Okay, I am going to go finish my shopping, if you wouldn't mind grabbing the chicken for me?"

I said, "No problem, I will get right on it."

I searched and searched.

Up and down the aisles I went, searching. She had decided upon getting a whole, breaded chicken, but no matter where I looked, I couldn't find it! I could have sworn it was in a particular place, but it wasn't. Even in the places I knew were outlandish, I checked anyway out of desperation! I was growing frustrated, tired, and, to be honest, scared and embarrassed. The only thing saving me was that this lady hadn't come looking for me yet, so I figured I still had some time to play it all off.

But then, to my dismay, she appeared. She looked tired. She found a seat in the store and sat down.

I apologized profusely! "I am so sorry; I could have sworn your chicken was right over here!"

She replied, "I know, right?"

I said, "Hold on, I found you something else that might work, but I'm not sure if it is enough...."

In my search, I saw a small pan of pre-cooked and pre-shredded chicken on a shelf somewhere. It looked open and picked through, but by then, I figured if she was desperate enough, she may want to settle for it. After showing this pan of chicken to her, it looked even more pathetic than I remembered!

I said, "This isn't enough, is it?" Shocked at myself that I would even consider this option!

In my dream, while I was frantically scouring the aisles, I passed by other workers and my manager several times.

I told the lady once more, "Please sit here, and I will be right back! I am going to ask someone!" She thought that was a good idea.

I awoke and the dream was over.

The idea struck me; I could have looked on the shopper app and found precisely what aisle the chicken was in. I also could have asked someone else for help.

The thought struck me all at once; there was a simple solution to this conundrum the whole time! How many times do we as Christians bang our heads against the wall doing things in our own strength? How many times do we scour this or that resource looking for answers to a challenging situation? How many times do we try and figure things out on our own? When there is a simple solution at our fingertips, should we simply choose to humble ourselves and ask?!

Listen, this was surely a crazy dream and probably fuelled by the protein bar I had right before bed, but nonetheless, it serves as a reminder that God so loves us, and He so desires to be a part of our lives! His word is a lamp unto our feet and a light unto our path, but only if we allow it to be! (See Psalm 119:105) We must invite God into our daily lives.

Rather than doing what we want to do in our own strength, we must come to a place of surrender, following His lead instead. His plans, His ways, His thoughts are so much higher, and He always knows what is best! Therefore, why not build a habit of running to Him right away, instead of far after the fact? After we have made a mess of things?

The good news is this: He is always there to help us and redeem us, but we don't always need to play catch up. If we learn to run to Him straightaway, doing things His way, we will begin to see victory in the areas we once thought were impossible!

God is for you, not against you!

Let Him be your guide!

Challenge Corner

- What are some areas in your life that you have been holding back from God? Perhaps you haven't been purposefully keeping Him at bay, but maybe there are things you have been doing on your own, in your own strength, that you could instead involve Him in?

_____

_____

_____

_____

_____

_____

_____

_____

_____

_____

_____

_____

_____

_____

_____

_____

_____

- What are some scriptures you can stand on today regarding putting God first? For example, let's suppose you are struggling with loving someone in your life. The Bible says we love because He first loved us! (See 1 John 4:19) What are some scriptures you can practically apply today to help you begin relying on the Lord's strength instead of your own?

_____

_____

_____

_____

Mornings with Jesus

"SEEK AND YOU SHALL FIND"

A	F	L	A	V	O	R	A	K	Z	L	M	H	G	B	T	U
W	W	V	Q	E	W	P	U	B	M	V	I	L	A	X	X	P
I	T	E	T	N	E	S	E	R	P	Y	H	P	A	N	R	T
S	E	X	S	I	Y	R	D	E	G	U	F	E	R	O	D	Y
H	C	F	T	O	V	X	F	S	E	R	A	P	S	S	N	S
E	A	S	O	K	M	L	L	L	O	R	T	N	O	C	V	H
D	F	S	Z	J	F	E	P	E	S	T	R	E	N	G	T	H
C	V	E	A	D	E	T	L	A	X	E	W	F	J	A	X	
M	R	R	N	T	B	V	B	V	T	Z	M	I	G	H	T	Y
K	G	T	F	E	E	E	G	D	E	L	W	O	N	K	C	A
B	J	S	X	E	S	C	O	V	L	X	Z	S	E	C	Y	L
D	E	P	Z	T	S	V	I	R	V	A	W	I	X	S	K	A
T	M	G	I	J	V	J	Z	T	Y	T	N	Q	G	S	R	O
E	S	L	O	W	D	O	W	N	C	E	R	U	S	H	E	D
E	L	P	Z	M	Z	L	U	Q	G	A	S	Q	D	A	S	K
F	N	J	B	S	N	O	I	T	A	N	R	M	A	L	E	V
Z	Q	Q	X	T	Z	N	J	O	J	G	A	P	H	C	V	O

Slow Down	Present	Flavor
Refuge	Exalted	Rushed
Nations	Mighty	Feet
Awesome	Practice	Control
Be Still	Strength	Stress
Genie	Spare	Facet
Wished	Acknowledge	Hands

"But rather seek ye the kingdom of God; and all these things shall be added unto you."
(Luke 12:31)

117

Never Let You Down
By: Joshua Scott Zeitz

Are you lost or lonely?
Feeling Overwhelmed?
Let the Bible be your compass!
Let Jesus take the helm!

Are you sinking in the deep?
Feel like your gonna drown?
Cry out to Jesus!
He'll never let you down!

Never Enough

"Philip answered, "Two hundred denarii (200 days' wages) worth of bread is not enough for each one to receive even a little." ~John 6:7 (AMP)

"There's not enough time, money, space, this or that..."

How many times have we caught ourselves saying these things when faced with an obstacle that, to us, seems insurmountable?

The disciples were faced with one such problem when they were gathered on the hillside and Jesus asked them what they should feed the multitude. Philip's answer: "There's not enough."

And I love how he didn't just say that, but he exaggerated his answer in an attempt to prove to Jesus just how extreme the situation was— as if Jesus didn't already realize a miracle was needed.

How many times do we do that very thing?

We need a new job, help finding a new house, help with a project, and help paying a bill. We begin to add up the numbers and quickly come to the conclusion that "Even if this, this, this, and this happens there won't be enough!"

And then we go to God with our Hail Mary prayers, "Oh God do you see how impossible this is?"

Listen, Jesus knew all along that a miracle was needed that day on the hillside, and He knew all along that He was going to take care of the whole thing. He was simply waiting for them to surrender their doubts and offer what they had.

Be encouraged today! God is more than enough! And He is able to do way more than you or I give Him credit for! He isn't looking for you to somehow figure out all the ins and outs and the details to every single facet of the situation you are in. He is waiting for you to come to Him with what you have, with a thankful heart, and offer it freely to Him.

"Lord, I know you are able. I know you are willing. I know that you care for me. Here I am, just as I am. I trust in you to take care of me! Thank you, Lord!!!"

God owns the cattle on a thousand hills. His driveway is solid gold. He is Alpha and Omega. He is more than enough!

Put your hope in Him today!

Hope is not wishing; it's a confident expectation of good!

Therefore, expect Good things today, because you serve a Good Father!

Expect Good things today, because you are a child of the King!

Expect Good things today, because you are adopted into the greatest family in the Universe!

Be encouraged! Don't look at what you can see or feel. Keep your eyes locked on Him, and He will make a way where there seems to be no way.

Be still and know that He is God.

He is more than enough!

> God can do in a moment,
> what we cannot in a lifetime!

Challenge Corner

- Have you ever gone to God telling Him why things won't work out? Telling Him how big your problem is? If so, you are not alone! We just read about the disciples and the feeding of the 5,000. We have all struggled with doubts, but be encouraged. God is more than enough, and He isn't thwarted because you and I have doubts or struggle with believing Him or taking Him at His Word. He is looking for availability, not ability. When we struggle to believe His promises, to believe He can and will make a way, the best thing we can do is to simply start believing Him! I know it sounds easy (and perhaps too good to be true), but the bottom line is that can't grow in our relationship with Him by wishing or trying, only by believing and doing! How can we show that we truly believe? Guard your hearts first and foremost and then guard your mouth! If you guard your heart, your mouth will catch up. In other words, what goes in, must come out, so be cautious and careful what you allow in! Let the Word of God dwell in you richly, so the Word of God comes out! (See Colossians 3:16)

- What are some practical steps you can take today to avoid allowing negative things and thoughts in your life?

_____

_____

_____

_____

_____

_____

_____

_____

_____

_____

_____

_____

_____

_____

_____

_____

_____

Continue...

Mornings with Jesus ☀

"SEEK AND YOU SHALL FIND"

E	Y	M	W	T	M	M	N	E	B	H	N	I	G	D	O	T
Z	X	T	Z	W	H	G	E	L	Q	E	N	M	N	E	E	M
I	N	X	J	B	O	D	L	B	A	X	Y	P	I	C	D	B
L	C	G	U	L	O	K	C	A	L	A	F	O	L	A	I	U
A	R	Z	D	W	B	C	A	T	L	G	M	S	L	F	S	Z
E	I	E	J	R	T	A	R	N	T	G	U	S	I	F	L	G
R	P	X	V	H	A	T	I	U	H	E	L	I	W	F	L	B
F	O	P	V	K	E	T	M	O	I	R	T	B	I	N	I	I
E	S	E	H	V	F	L	B	M	N	A	I	L	C	V	H	Q
L	S	C	E	N	L	E	K	R	G	T	T	E	V	M	Y	D
C	I	T	L	D	O	C	B	U	S	E	U	Z	Z	F	O	Q
A	B	P	P	E	F	C	W	S	S	D	D	D	E	U	F	V
T	L	I	T	A	N	X	L	N	K	G	E	X	B	R	W	Z
S	E	L	Q	W	B	O	L	I	M	X	Y	T	V	S	O	H
B	S	I	T	D	Z	F	U	V	E	R	S	I	F	Y	I	M
O	Y	H	P	U	T	K	N	G	K	C	R	F	R	D	K	C
Y	U	P	D	I	E	A	Z	W	H	N	C	Q	A	R	Q	F

Hillside	Miracle	Willing
Enough	Help	Cattle
Exaggerated	Philip	Gold
Obstacle	Doubts	Expect
Multitude	Insurmountable	All Things
Feat	Impossible	Possible
Faced	Realize	More

"Get wisdom, get understanding: forget it not; neither decline from the words of my mouth. Forsake her not, and she shall preserve thee: love her, and she shall keep thee."
(Proverbs 4:5,6)

123

Waiting

By: Joshua Scott Zeitz

Losing hope,
waning fast,
I just don't know
how long I'll last,
waiting for Your Word
to come to pass.

Hoping and wishing,
I keep reminiscing
the past.
You've done it before,
You'll do it again!
I'm holding on,
but I don't know when...

Is this a dream?
Is this pretend?
Is this false hope?
Is this the end?

I've seen Your work,
I've read Your plays.
I know Your heart,
I know Your ways.

Even if...

You never change!

Even if...

For all my days,

Even if...

I'll give You praise!

An Excellent Spirit

"A wise man will hear and will increase learning; And a man of understanding shall attain unto wise counsels: The fear of the LORD is the beginning of knowledge: But fools despise wisdom and instruction." ~Proverbs 1:5-7 (KJV)

In Daniel chapter 1, Daniel and his three companions, Hananiah, Mishaal, and Azariah, spent much time being prepared for what was to come in subsequent chapters. Preparation time is never wasted time and a man's gifts will bring him before great men! (See Proverbs 18:16)

At the beginning of chapter 2, King Nebuchadnezzar dreamed dreams which highly troubled him, to the point that he called for his crew of magicians, soothsayers, and astrologers to make the dreams known to him.

However, there was a major twist that they were not expecting. Not only did he ask them to interpret the dream, but he expected them to tell the King the contents of the dream without him first telling them about it. In other words, he asked them to do an impossible thing!

Unable to give the king all that he desired, the entire group of magicians, soothsayers, and astrologers was sentenced to death. However, Daniel heard of the decree of death and sought wisely to speak with the man who was charged with the task of carrying out the sentence.

Upon hearing why the King was so angry and sought in haste to kill everyone in the magician's school, Daniel implored the king to grant some time to him and his three companions so they could reveal both the dream and its interpretation.

Listen to what Daniel and his three companions did:

"Then Daniel returned to his house and discussed the matter with Hananiah, Mishaal, and Azariah, his companions, in order that they might seek compassion from the God of heaven regarding this secret, so that Daniel and his companions would not be executed with the rest of the wise men of Babylon." ~Daniel 2:17-18 (AMP)

Notice Daniel and the three didn't run to their books or their scrolls, nor did they rely on their learning in any manner. Instead, they ran to God, the One who can make all things possible, and sought His help, His compassion!

The fear of the LORD is the beginning of knowledge…

The secret was then revealed to Daniel in a vision of the night! What an awesome God we serve!

Once Daniel received the vision, he could have gotten puffed up with pride, gone before the king in arrogance, and demanded the death of everyone except him and his companions, taking credit for what God alone deserved. But he didn't do any of that. Instead, he gave God all the glory, praising Him and thanking Him in a most magnificent way! (See Daniel 2:20-23)

Daniel first sought to save the lives of all the wise men of Babylon, and then he was brought before the king regarding the king's dream.

Daniel made no attempt to hide the impossibility of the king's request, declaring boldly, "But there is a God in heaven who reveals secrets…"

Listen to Daniel's amazing and humble response to the king:

"But as for me, this secret has not been revealed to me because my wisdom is greater than that of any other living man, but in order to make the interpretation known to the king, and so you may fully understand the thoughts of your mind." ~Daniel 2:30 (AMP)

In other words, "It's not about me, king! God wanted to make this dream known to you and he allowed me to know it, but I am not the wise one here, He is!"

Wow! There is so much packed within these 30 verses, and we can glean so much from how Daniel responded to the situation: how he wisely sought counsel from his companions, how he wisely sought counsel from the king's bodyguard, how he wisely sought time to interpret the dream from the king, and so forth.

However, what I want to draw attention to is how he wisely humbled himself before the King of kings and Lord of lords!

Listen, no matter what you are facing today, God is good, and He is good all the time! He desires to make things known to us! He does not hide things from us, but rather for us.

The way to unlock and unveil the things He has for us is by being humble. Humbling ourselves under His mighty hand, under His Word, is the key to bringing about His wisdom, favor, and knowledge in our lives!

No matter what you are facing today or in the future, make a habit right now of putting Him first, of acknowledging Him in all your ways, of surrendering your life, your thoughts, to Him!

And then, give Him all the glory when He comes through and works the impossible in your life!

Daniel could have gloated and taken credit for the vision, but how long would that pride have carried him? What would happen when the next problem arises? The next dream? The next challenge? Who would he call on then if he spent all his time riding the waves of past successes puffed up with pride?

It is imperative that we live in that realm of humility before the Lord!

Take some time today to seek the Lord with all your heart! Put others first. Seek to *serve* rather than to be served, and watch how God shows up in ways you never thought possible.

He loves to show out on the behalf of the humble!

Challenge Corner

- How did Daniel exhibit humility?

_____

_____

_____

_____

_____

_____

_____

_____

_____

_____

_____

_____

_____

- How can we emulate what he did in our everyday lives?

_____

_____

_____

_____

_____

_____

_____

_____

_____

_____

_____

_____

_____

_____

_____

_____

- Doing things with a spirit of excellence is a good thing. However, pushing past excellence to perfection and then taking credit for the work with things like, "I am self-made," is a pitfall. Remember, even the devil was a beautiful angel at one point, until pride was found in him. It is imperative that we learn to live in a state of humility, giving God the glory and credit He so wonderfully deserves!

- In your own words, what does it mean to walk and live in humility? (Hint: Humility is not about never being seen, or stepping out, but rather about doing things God's way and giving Him all the glory!)

_____
_____
_____
_____
_____
_____
_____
_____
_____
_____
_____
_____
_____
_____
_____
_____
_____
_____
_____
_____
_____

To Be A Servant
By: Isaiah Joshua Zeitz

"And whatever you do, do it heartily, as to the Lord and not to men," ~Colossians 3:23 (NKJV)

Jesus was the greatest example of being a servant. It says in John 13:5 (NKJV); *"After that, He poured water into a basin and began to wash the disciples' feet, and to wipe them with the towel..."*

Wow! Jesus washed His disciple's dirty feet! THAT is being a true servant.

God Himself came to serve not to be served, and it says in John 13:15 (NKJV); *"For I have given you an example, that you should do as I have done to you."*

Jesus always put others before Himself. He never sought the spotlight.

He gave us an awesome example to follow, and the good news is He gives us the power to be like Him!

In Christ,

Isaiah Joshua Zeitz

Challenge Corner

- Do you struggle with being a servant?

_____

_____

_____

_____

_____

_____

_____

_____

_____

_____

_____

- Or do you tend to seek the spotlight?

_____

_____

_____

_____

_____

_____

_____

_____

_____

_____

_____

_____

_____

_____

_____

_____

Mornings with Jesus

"SEEK AND YOU SHALL FIND"

G	W	U	M	O	D	S	I	W	M	O	T	T	N	N	O	T
S	Y	N	K	E	G	R	A	H	C	Q	O	O	O	G	J	Q
B	N	L	H	C	R	U	Q	V	I	M	I	L	J	D	V
I	O	O	I	O	W	Q	I	P	U	T	T	E	A	E	K	K
Q	T	C	I	T	G	W	J	O	A	C	A	T	W	C	G	S
V	S	K	Z	N	V	E	Y	R	U	N	J	C	K	X	S	B
N	E	E	L	Z	A	K	A	R	K	O	A	G	U	V	E	R
O	L	C	B	C	S	P	T	H	E	X	C	C	Q	A	E	E
I	B	N	O	B	E	S	M	L	L	S	K	O	O	B	K	V
S	M	E	C	R	N	S	C	O	E	Q	M	M	L	W	Q	O
S	U	T	P	I	C	O	Z	N	C	F	T	A	I	V	I	R
A	H	N	I	H	U	Z	Y	A	T	E	R	C	E	S	B	P
P	D	E	C	N	L	V	X	E	C	V	T	C	W	R	W	Z
M	N	S	S	I	R	K	J	T	K	J	Z	K	A	S	D	U
O	Y	E	D	D	A	N	I	E	L	U	G	H	R	G	C	L
C	L	K	V	I	S	I	O	N	S	L	L	O	R	C	S	Z
Q	T	V	N	O	I	T	A	T	E	R	P	R	E	T	N	I

Wisdom
Preparation
Proverbs
Charge
Dream
Compassion
Books

Interpretation
Instruction
Sentence
Companions
Scrolls
Secret
Vision

Daniel
Glean
Key
Humble
Seek
Unlock
Counsel

"and whatsoever ye do, do it heartily, as to the Lord, and not unto men;"
(Colossians 3:23)

Enough is Enough

"Therefore, since we are surrounded by so great a cloud of witnesses [who by faith have testified to the truth of God's absolute faithfulness], *stripping off every unnecessary weight and the sin which so easily and cleverly entangles us, let us run with endurance and active persistence the race that is set before us,"* ~Hebrews 12:1 (AMP)

Something that I used to struggle with quite a lot was beating myself up, not recognizing who I was in Christ. This caused me to constantly go back into things that I had already been freed from because I felt like, "What's the point? I'm a nobody anyway!"

My pastor said something a little while back that really resonated in my spirit. He said, "I need you to be free."

"Be free!"

There is so much packed into those two little words! Think about it - if you are asking someone to "be," then they already possess the tools and resources to do so.

Simply put, "be" means it's already done!

Be encouraged today, I have awesome news for you, Jesus paid it all on the cross! He didn't just pay for our sin, He paid for our joy, peace, healing, victory, favor, and so much more! He did His part, and our part is to "be" all that He paid for us to be, which in simplified terms is completely free!

Free from fear, free from worry, free from sickness, free from shame, guilt, anger, jealousy, wickedness, addiction, poverty, you name it, He paid it!

Listen, for so many years I struggled with my identity, and even now every once in a while, an old thought or demon tries to come knocking, but can I tell you the ultimate and easiest way to be free?

Immerse yourself in the Word of God! Immerse yourself in what He has to say about you!

Did you know that He is always thinking good things about you?

I have heard my pastor say this before as well, "If God had a fridge, your picture would be on it! If God drove a car, your bumper sticker would be on it!" Imagine that: God driving around in a minivan with "Father of (insert your name), my beloved!"

It may seem far-fetched, and if you are prone to deal with the same things I did and still have to stave off continually with the Word, then you are going to have a tougher time than most seeing yourself as the apple of God's eye. But I want to encourage you today - you are!

Perhaps you grew up in a home with very little love and affection or positive affirmation and you feel like an orphan most days. Can I tell you some more good news? You have been adopted into the greatest Family there is! You are accepted by the Best, who cares about the rest!

You are who He says you are!

Enough is enough! Draw a line in the spiritual sand today and declare to yourself, the world, the devil, that you are no longer going to allow past faults to define you. You aren't going to allow the things that Jesus paid for to weigh you down any longer. In Jesus' name, you have the power and authority to cast them off and be free!

You are not defined by what you do or what you did; you are defined by who you are: a child of the King!

When we immerse ourselves in the Word on a continual basis, what we do, say, and think will begin to line up with the Word, and we will walk with a new confidence being able to rightly share the gospel with others because we know who we are. We are free!

Go ahead, right now where you are; begin to thank Him for what He has done for you! Thank Him for who He is and who He has made you!

"Thank you, Lord, for the price you paid for me. Thank you that I am redeemed. I am whole! I am healed! I am free! I am yours! I am adopted! I have peace! I have joy! Because of you Lord! Thank you! In Jesus' name!"

Challenge Corner

• How do you think God views you? What thoughts does He think about you? Do you think He ever thinks about you?

_____
_____
_____
_____
_____
_____
_____
_____
_____
_____
_____
_____
_____
_____
_____
_____
_____
_____
_____
_____

- How do you see Him? What thoughts do you think about Him?

_____
_____
_____
_____
_____
_____
_____
_____
_____
_____
_____
_____
_____
_____
_____
_____
_____
_____
_____
_____
_____
_____
_____
_____
_____
_____
_____
_____
_____
_____

- The next time discouragement tries to overtake you, encourage someone else! Write them a letter, send them a text, give them a hug, cook them a meal. The possibilities are endless. Remember: What we make happen for others, God will make happen for us!

- What has the Lord done for you? Make a list. Thank Him on a regular basis for those things. The next time discouragement tries to overtake you, look at that list.

_____

_____

_____

_____

_____

_____

_____

_____

_____

_____

_____

_____

_____

_____

_____

_____

_____

_____

_____

_____

_____

_____

You are not defined by what you do
or what you did;
you are defined by who you are:
a child of the King!

Mornings with Jesus

"SEEK AND YOU SHALL FIND"

B	Z	Q	E	N	I	L	A	W	A	R	D	Q	P	I	O	C
U	L	H	Z	Q	L	C	K	D	E	F	I	N	E	D	M	E
T	P	P	P	Y	V	T	I	Z	B	Q	D	R	M	M	X	B
O	W	C	J	Q	N	O	I	T	A	M	R	I	F	F	A	L
H	P	C	U	M	I	N	I	V	A	N	H	P	V	G	F	Q
Y	A	M	I	H	K	N	A	H	T	D	E	T	P	O	D	A
X	I	E	N	O	U	G	H	F	R	I	D	G	E	D	Y	S
D	D	L	B	U	X	E	L	P	P	A	G	J	A	E	O	M
E	F	M	E	N	T	A	N	G	L	E	S	C	C	R	E	R
V	O	A	E	U	V	N	S	J	O	N	C	N	P	I	V	C
O	R	J	M	E	V	C	D	H	M	E	E	H	E	D	I	L
L	D	O	D	I	R	M	S	W	P	D	A	S	A	E	T	O
E	E	T	I	N	L	F	F	T	I	N	R	P	M	N	I	U
B	B	F	C	G	Y	Y	E	F	V	E	L	Z	L	T	S	D
C	D	W	R	C	P	D	N	B	M	C	A	V	K	I	O	Z
X	G	U	U	R	Q	O	L	M	N	B	M	A	N	T	P	U
B	M	E	T	W	C	E	I	M	B	D	C	A	J	Y	W	F

Enough	Paid For	Apple
Cloud	Entangles	Affirmation
Be Free	Immerse	Defined
Identity	Beloved	Draw A Line
Orphan	Positive	Accepted
Adopted	Thank Him	Fridge
Family	Confidence	Minivan

"Be careful for nothing; but in every thing by prayer and supplication with thanksgiving let your requests be made known to God."
(Philippians 4:6)

Come Holy Spirit

By: Joshua Scott Zeitz

Come Holy Spirit,
Come fill this place,
with Your lovingkindness,
Your mercy and grace!
Mold me and make me,
Come have Your way!
Come Holy Spirit,
Come have this space!
This is Your moment,
Your secret place!
Come Holy Spirit,
Come have Your way!

Break Through

"Now Joshua had commanded the people, saying, "You shall not shout or make any noise with your voice, nor shall a word proceed out of your mouth, until the day I say to you, 'Shout!' Then you shall shout."" ~Joshua 6:10 (NKJV)

Christianity is less about performance and all about position. The position I am talking about is not the same as the world talks about, however. The world wants us to be constantly vying for position by being the loudest in the room, making ourselves known, and getting people to pay attention to us.

God's Kingdom is contrary to the world. Jesus said the greatest in the Kingdom is the greatest servant. The way to move "up" in God's family, is by serving others, putting others first!

In essence, the way up, is down.

Jesus says there is no greater gift that a man can give than to lay down his life for his friends! (See John 15:13)

Think about that. Jesus has always been God; long before He became Jesus, He already had heaven, glory, fame, streets of gold, and so much more...

He gave it all up to win us back from the enemy, from sin! He is our example of what it means to lay down one's life.

Listen; there are so many distractions in this world. The enemy wants to pull you off God's assignment for you! The distractions and temptations are meant to steal, kill, and destroy us. They are meant to get us over in the realm of the world saying, "Look at me! Look at me!"

The Holy Spirit, however, will always lead us to a place of "Look at Him! Look at Him!"

Why? Because God always desires the best for us, and He knows things we don't. He sees the end from the beginning! (See Isaiah 46:10)

Be encouraged today! Don't allow the distractions of this world to take you off course, to steal your joy, to get you thinking only about yourself.

The good news is this: You can start today!

Reach out to someone today. Ask the Lord, "What would you have me do today?"

Joshua told the people; only shout when I tell you to. If they would have disobeyed at any point, that wall would not have come down.

God wants to see you have your breakthrough, but be encouraged, His timing is always perfect! Trust it.

Learn to cherish the waiting with Him! Learn to cherish the small acts of obedience. Shout when He says shout, and you will see your breakthrough!

Challenge Corner

- It's the small acts of obedience that often lead to great victories! When was the last time the Lord spoke to you to do something? What did you do? Did you obey? If not, don't beat yourself up! God isn't about shaming us or only giving us one chance. The best thing we can do…make the next right choice!

_____

_____

_____

_____

_____

_____

- Have you ever felt the pressure to fit in? To vie for position? To do something that perhaps you knew wasn't right or didn't feel right in order to fit in or to be accepted? What was your reaction? How did you handle the situation?

_____

_____

_____

_____

_____

_____

_____

_____

_____

_____

_____

_____

_____

_____

_____

_____

_____

_____

_____

_____

_____

_____

_____

_____

- We mustn't try to fit God into our little boxes or ways of thinking. The Bible says His ways and thoughts are higher than ours! Therefore, the best thing we can do is follow His lead, and never belittle the little! It's the little acts of obedience that position us to receive from Him and give to others.

- Are you believing God for a breakthrough in your life? Remember, He uses people! So, make a habit of walking through crowds slowly; your breakthrough may come sooner than you think!

_____

_____

_____

_____

_____

_____

_____

_____

_____

_____

_____

_____

_____

_____

_____

_____

_____

_____

_____

_____

_____

_____

_____

_____

_____

_____

_____

_____

_____

_____

Mornings with Jesus

"SEEK AND YOU SHALL FIND"

F	R	Y	O	D	Z	H	F	C	B	Z	P	B	D	D	W
R	F	L	G	X	Q	A	R	D	R	V	Y	C	E	L	O	S
C	G	F	U	D	C	V	E	H	E	D	P	H	C	R	O	U
M	Y	W	K	A	H	R	U	L	G	C	E	I	L	O	P	W
O	A	D	D	Z	E	T	B	M	B	B	O	E	A	W	P	G
R	P	E	O	F	N	A	W	M	Z	L	P	P	R	H	O	F
E	S	V	F	E	R	T	R	A	E	H	L	V	E	E	R	Y
L	F	O	M	E	W	S	K	T	K	N	E	J	N	I	T	T
W	K	O	N	S	P	F	S	T	R	O	F	M	O	C	U	I
N	M	L	O	C	T	E	T	E	Z	O	R	O	K	U	N	L
M	U	G	C	B	Y	K	Y	R	Y	W	R	D	K	P	I	I
V	B	E	L	B	A	U	L	A	V	T	O	R	Q	X	T	M
S	E	G	A	R	U	O	C	N	E	T	E	E	E	J	I	U
G	E	G	N	E	L	L	A	H	C	B	T	I	C	B	E	H
T	E	S	T	I	F	I	E	D	R	K	L	R	C	F	S	D
Z	Q	A	D	L	G	E	D	I	S	N	I	X	Z	O	T	T
O	V	I	C	T	O	R	I	E	S	S	H	A	R	E	S	K

Breakthrough	Gift	Realm
Position	Timing	Joshua
Attention	Perfect	Reach Out
Distractions	Cherish	Look At Me
Vying	Performance	World
Servant	Obedience	Course
Greater	Contrary	Look At Him

"And we know that all things work together for good to them that love God, to them who are called according to his purpose."
(Romans 8:28)

Free

By: Joshua Scott Zeitz

This aint mom's spaghetti,
more like pops' lasagna,
frontin free in the flows,
got you out of your genre!
I spit bars harder
than 8 miles of llamas!
I'm reppin for Christ,
but you're just stuck on the commas!
Fumbling them lyrics,
worser than Tony Romo,
rappin bout chains,
got you soundin like a FOMO!
I'd rather spit clean,
acquiesce as a SLOMO,
than sell my soul for likes,
off the dome for a PROMO!
Livin for the now,
shallow mottos like, YOLO?!
Short-lived success,
got you sleepin like a DODO!

Livin in the past,
chasin reels like a PHOTO!
A slave to the pressure,
so depressed like FRODO!
Dressed to impress,
but repressed on the LOLO!
Desperate for attention,
got you bummin like a HOBO!
I gotta keep it real,
all this posin is a NOGO!
Pushin poison on the mic,
got you slinkin like a YOYO!
Here today, gone tomorrow,
got your life like a POGO!
I'd rather be free,
lookin like QuasiMODO,
than turnin tricks for trolls,
livin life on the LOCO!
Engulfed with them dubs,
bowin down to a LOGO?!
I'm FREE!

Enduring Love

"Looking unto Jesus
the author and finisher of our faith,
who for the joy that was set before him
endured the cross,
despising the shame,
and is set down at the right hand
of the throne of God."

~Hebrews 12:2 (KJV)

Today I want to focus on an often forgotten but powerful part of the crucifixion that Jesus did for us! When we think about the cross and the crucifixion, and the entire passion really, what comes to mind? The torturous whipping? The crown of thorns? The nails being driven into His hands and feet? His beard being ripped off? His body being marred beyond recognition?

Listen, Jesus endured the most excruciatingly painful death for us! There is no question about it. Also consider this: it pleased the Father to bruise Him on our behalf! Why? Because this was God's plan from the moment Adam and Eve committed high treason. God knew this would have to be done, and He waited until the perfect moment in time, when crucifixion was a thing, to bring about the birth of Jesus, so that Jesus could die in such a manner.

Anyone else would have died after undergoing such pain, or at the very least, passed out under the strain of it all, but Jesus was not only fully man, but also fully God! He endured to the end!

His enduring Love for you and me overwhelmed Him! The Bible says it was the joy that was set before Him that caused Him to endure. What an awesome God we serve!

His enduring Love propelled Him to not only die in the most agonizing of ways, but also to suffer the shame of the cross. The cross was considered a curse. It was the most shameful way to die. Our Lord was hung naked on a tree outside of town, while Roman soldiers mocked Him and cast lots for His robes.

As He hung there, gasping for air, you and I were on His mind! His Love was so enduring that He made time to invite the repentant thief into glory with Him, to ask forgiveness for the very ones mocking Him at His feet, to unite John and His mother.

He could have, at any moment, called upon a score of angels to rescue Him and exact revenge on the ones who hung Him there. But His enduring Love propelled Him to go forward and fulfill all of scripture! No man took His life, He laid it down!

What an awesome God we serve!

No matter what you are facing today or ever, remember what Jesus did for you. Remember the shame of it all, the humiliation He endured: To be stripped naked and hung on a tree in front of His disciples, His mother, His Father, His followers, His people, His enemies…

He endured the cross for us!

We were the joy set before Him!

The next time we are tempted to focus only on our problems, our trials, our mess, look to the cross and remember His enduring Love!

God loves you so much,
more than you know!

Challenge Corner

- What does the cross mean to you? What does it represent in your life?

_____

_____

_____

_____

_____

_____

_____

_____

_____

_____

_____

_____

_____

_____

_____

_____

- Honesty moment: How often have you thought about the cross? About what Jesus had to endure upon it?

_____

_____

_____

_____

_____

_____

- One of my favorite songs is "The Old Rugged Cross." How can we better incorporate its message, what it stands for, into our everyday lives?

_____

_____

_____

_____

_____

_____

_____

_____

_____

_____

_____

_____

_____

_____

_____

_____

- The Bible says we are to take up our cross daily. What does that mean?

_____

_____

_____

_____

_____

_____

_____

_____

_____

_____

_____

_____

_____

_____

_____

_____

- Remember: To avoid the ditch, don't get hung up on images or items. It's not the physical cross we should be focusing on. It's not about hanging a cross in our home or church. It's about the message. Just like a Bible, it isn't holy in and of itself. The Bible is just a bunch of paper and bindings. But the message found within, and applying that message, changes us for eternity! How have you been changed today?

_____

_____

_____

_____

_____

_____

_____

_____

_____

_____

_____

_____

_____

_____

_____

_____

_____

_____

_____

_____

_____

God didn't just call you valuable; He showed you your value by laying down His life for you!

Mornings with Jesus

"SEEK AND YOU SHALL FIND"

F	R	Y	O	D	Z	H	F	C	B	Z	P	B	D	D	D	W
R	F	L	G	X	Q	A	R	D	R	V	Y	C	E	L	O	S
C	G	F	U	D	C	V	E	H	E	D	P	H	C	R	O	U
M	Y	W	K	A	H	R	U	L	G	C	E	I	L	O	P	W
O	A	D	D	Z	E	T	B	M	B	B	O	E	A	W	P	G
R	P	E	O	F	N	A	W	M	Z	L	P	P	R	H	O	F
E	S	V	F	E	R	T	R	A	E	H	L	V	E	E	R	Y
L	F	O	M	E	W	S	K	T	K	N	E	J	N	I	T	T
W	K	O	N	S	P	F	S	T	R	O	F	M	O	C	U	I
N	M	L	O	C	T	E	T	E	Z	O	R	O	K	U	N	L
M	U	G	C	B	Y	K	Y	R	Y	W	R	D	K	P	I	I
V	B	E	L	B	A	U	L	A	V	T	O	R	Q	X	T	M
S	E	G	A	R	U	O	C	N	E	T	E	E	E	J	I	U
G	E	G	N	E	L	L	A	H	C	B	T	I	C	B	E	H
T	E	S	T	I	F	I	E	D	R	K	L	R	C	F	S	D
Z	Q	A	D	L	G	E	D	I	S	N	I	X	Z	O	T	T
O	V	I	C	T	O	R	I	E	S	S	H	A	R	E	S	K

Breakthrough	Gift	Realm
Position	Timing	Joshua
Attention	Perfect	Reach Out
Distractions	Cherish	Look At Me
Vying	Performance	World
Servant	Obedience	Course
Greater	Contrary	Look At Him

"And we know that all things work together for good to them that love God, to them who are called according to his purpose."
(Romans 8:28)

My Super Girl

By: Joshua Scott Zeitz
(Written for the love of my life, Mitzi)

"Whoso findeth a wife
findeth a good thing,
and obtaineth favour of the Lord."
~Proverbs 18:22 (KJV)

my super girl
with your super smile
take my hand
and sit awhile
with me
come sit awhile with me

tell me about your day
tell me about the way
you rode upon the waves
you make the world great
I thank the Lord for you
with you I'm not afraid
with you I find my strength
I love the way you love me

I love the way you care
I love the way you hold me
run your fingers through my hair
we share our hopes
we share our dreams
we share our home
we share our things
I thank the Lord for you
come sit awhile with me
please sit awhile with me

my super girl
with your super smile
take my hand
and sit awhile
with me
come sit awhile with me

we've made so many memories
adventures come and gone
you've always stood right by me
it's made our love so strong
the pitter patter playing
it doesn't last for long
I'll cherish it forever

it's why I wrote this song
I know the time is coming
to give their hands away
I thank the Lord for you girl
take my hand, lets pray
come sit awhile with me
please sit awhile with me

my super girl
with your super smile
take my hand
and sit awhile
with me
come sit awhile with me

the halls are filled with laughter
as children's children play
I sit and watch the smile
beam across your face
silver hair and laugh lines
your beauty still remains
I thank the Lord for you girl
my love for you's the same
come sit awhile with me
please sit awhile with me

we once were young
and now we're old
take my hand and lead me home
the lights grow dim
I'm getting cold
sit awhile with me
come sit awhile with me

my super girl
with your super smile
take my hand
and sit awhile
with me
come sit awhile with me...

Yours Eternally,
Joshua

Man's Empty Praise

"But whatever former things were gains to me [as I thought then], *these things* [once regarded as advancements in merit] *I have come to consider as loss* [absolutely worthless] *for the sake of Christ* [and the purpose which He has given my life].

But more than that, I count everything as loss compared to the priceless privilege and supreme advantage of knowing Christ Jesus my Lord [and of growing more deeply and thoroughly acquainted with Him—a joy unequaled]. *For His sake I have lost everything, and I consider it all garbage, so that I may gain Christ, and may be found in Him* [believing in and relying on Him], *not having any righteousness of my own derived from* [my obedience to] *the Law and its rituals, but* [possessing] *that* [genuine righteousness] *which comes through faith in Christ, the righteousness which comes from God on the basis of faith."* ~Philippians 3:7-9 (AMP)

I love the Bible!

It needs no interpretation! It needs no man to come along and say things like, "This is what this passage means to me," or "This is what this is truly saying right here." Instead, when taken at face value, the Bible is an amazingly awesome and simple book to understand, free from any contradictions. God designed it that way!

Where we get in trouble with the Bible, is not with the Bible itself or its supposed complexity or hard-to-grasp truths, but rather when we attempt to weave our self-worth, our own self-righteousness within its pages.

Take, for instance, an individual that is not born-again, who has not received the Spirit of God, and who has not yet been adopted into the family of God. This person is not going to grasp the Bible at all! They are going to make all kinds of wild accusations against it, because they have zero ability to comprehend the truths found within. They are going to be hard-pressed to believe that any of the miracles were real, that any of the beasts or fantastical creatures found within are anything more than stories derived from man's imagination.

Next let's take a look at the morally devout "religious" person. This person may or may not have had an experience with the True and Living God, but for whatever reason, they surely don't believe everything in the Bible. They see it more as a guidebook, a book of wildly imaginative stories yes, but more than that, a book that helps one walk the straight and narrow.

David and Goliath? Samson? Jonah and the whale? Daniel and the lion's den? Let's not even start with the book of Revelation!

These are amazing stories, where we can interject ourselves into the pages, and present ourselves as the hero or heroine, but they are really nothing more than that: stories.

The morally devout "religious" person reads the Bible not to be changed, but rather to see how the writings can make them even better, how the stories within can relate to them, how they can make them a better version of themselves!

Listen, I am not going to presume to know all the inner workings of the mind of man. Nor would it be wise to assume to know what any given person is thinking at all times regarding the Bible. I simply intend to paint something that is entirely obtuse, something rather extreme, so we can clearly see the other side of things.

Take for example Paul.

Within the pages of chapter 3 of the book of Philippians, Paul paints a picture of his own self-worth, his own self-righteousness, naming off a list of things that many in his day and time would have considered quite praiseworthy. However, Paul then goes on to say that all these things, these things that he supposedly gained, were really not gains at all, but rather a big pile of garbage!

For that matter, ANYTHING that doesn't have to do with

knowing Christ, he considers worthy of the dung heap!

I want to take a moment and ask you a question, to present a challenge to not only you, but me as well…

Have we reached that point in our walk with the Lord?

What is most important to us: When we read the Bible, do we read it with an air of self-importance, to simply live lives to our already-brimming-with-righteousness?

Or do we possess the attitude of David when he said, *"As the deer pants for the water brooks, so pants my soul for You, oh God!"* ~Psalm 42:1 (NKJV)

Or what about Job, *"I have not departed from the commandment of His lips; I have treasured the words of His mouth more than my necessary food."* ~Job 23:12 (NKJV)

Or what about Paul once again? *"For to me, to live is Christ* [He is my source of joy, my reason to live] *and to die is gain* [for I will be with Him in eternity]." ~Philippians 1:21 (AMP)

Listen, today's word of encouragement is not meant to condemn or brow-beat at all, but rather to serve as a point of perspective.

When I look out at the world, and I see the atrocities that are happening all around us, I can't help but think, if not but for the grace of God, there go I…

Paul, David, Job, and so many others in the Bible, knew what it was like to come to the end of themselves, to taste the bitterness of self-righteousness, of self-reliance, of self-worth in and of itself. And each of these men—and so many men and women like them - came to realize that without Christ, they were nothing!

The older in the Lord that I get, the more I am coming to realize that without Him, I am nothing!

Before Jesus, I was an absolute mess, a train-wreck, a sinful and wicked individual who not only practiced wicked things, but loved them.

Now I am born-again! I am a new creature! The things that used to appeal to me, the things that I used to derive pleasure and meaning from, they are garbage to me now! BUT I still need Him. Every hour, every moment, I need Him!

What about you?

"My soul thirsts for God, for the living God. When shall I appear before God?" ~Psalm 42:2 (NKJV)

"O God, You are my God; Early will I seek You; My soul thirsts for You In a dry and thirsty land Where there is no water. So have I looked for You in the sanctuary, To see Your power and Your glory. Because Your lovingkindness is better than life, My lips shall praise You." ~Psalm 63:1-3 (NKJV)

Challenge Corner

• Look up Ephesians 2:8-9 and compare it to the above passage, Philippians 3:7-9. What are the similarities between these verses?

_____

_____

_____

_____

_____

_____

_____

_____

_____

_____

_____

_____

_____

_____

- How can we apply them to our lives to help us gain a better understanding of where our righteousness comes from?

_____

_____

_____

_____

_____

_____

_____

_____

_____

_____

_____

_____

_____

- How can we then use this knowledge to better witness to others about Jesus?

_____

_____

_____

_____

_____

_____

_____

_____

_____

_____

_____

_____

_____

_____

_____

_____

- Saul (before he was Paul) was killing Christians in the name of God! He had a self-proclaimed righteousness. What changed in him after the Damascus road experience? [Hint: He was born-again! Read II Corinthians 5:17. This radical transformation takes place on the inside of every person when they get born-again. Then after that, as they walk with the Lord, renewing their minds to the Word of God, we begin to see the fruit manifested in their lives as a direct result of that internal change.]

_____

_____

_____

_____

_____

_____

_____

_____

_____

_____

_____

_____

_____

_____

_____

_____

_____

_____

_____

_____

_____

- On a scale of 1-10, (1 being poor and 10 being excellent), how would you rate your walk with the Lord right now in terms of proclaiming your own righteousness versus putting all your hope and trust in Him?

  1   2   3   4   5   6   7   8   9   10

- Something to keep in mind (especially when we have been saved for quite some time and living in the church world for quite some time) is that it can be easy to forget where the Lord found us. The Bible says that without Him, we can do nothing! But, through Him, we can do all things! Concerning our ministry to others, especially those who are new Christians or those who have never been exposed to church, it is important to keep our relationship with the Lord fresh, remembering daily His goodness! Remember this tenet: If but by the grace of God, there go I! We all need a daily reliance on the Lord and His strength, never our own.

I'd rather get a crown from Jesus,
than a Grammy from man!

Mornings with Jesus

"SEEK AND YOU SHALL FIND"

U	B	T	X	S	E	I	R	O	T	S	U	B	K	J	Z	S
N	B	H	R	U	Y	I	V	U	D	P	S	H	B	D	H	G
Y	O	G	J	E	S	O	B	M	S	C	L	F	O	A	S	N
G	U	I	D	E	B	O	O	K	U	P	K	V	R	V	U	I
G	N	X	J	V	F	U	M	E	K	F	D	E	N	I	P	H
S	U	O	I	G	I	L	E	R	P	U	N	U	A	D	R	T
V	I	N	P	R	H	T	A	I	L	O	G	F	G	Q	E	R
K	L	A	O	P	O	I	S	O	F	J	H	I	A	F	M	E
J	U	X	W	O	R	T	H	L	E	S	S	C	I	J	E	M
L	N	O	S	M	A	S	M	W	E	N	I	U	N	E	G	R
Z	I	N	T	E	R	P	R	E	T	A	T	I	O	N	I	O
I	Y	I	S	E	L	F	W	O	R	T	H	C	I	Y	K	F
Z	G	X	E	A	E	V	I	T	A	N	I	G	A	M	I	W
M	A	C	C	U	S	A	T	I	O	N	S	Y	G	P	F	D
P	R	I	C	E	L	E	S	S	S	O	L	L	W	A	T
D	E	N	I	A	G	W	H	O	D	Y	T	S	R	I	H	T
X	T	Z	G	A	R	B	A	G	E	B	U	F	I	B	N	G

Religious   Gained   David
Born Again   Worthless   Imaginative
Interpretation Samson   Former Things
Supreme   Accusations   Goliath
Loss   Guidebook   Stories
Paul   Priceless   Self Worth
Genuine   Garbage   Thirsty

For by grace are ye saved
through faith; and that not of
yourselves: it is the gift of God:
Not of works, lest any man should
boast.
(Ephesians 2:8,9)

God Man

By: Joshua Scott Zeitz

Some are self-made men,
I'm a God-made man!
Some say self only wins,
I'm on God-laid plans!
Some claim self-taught ends,
I'm like, "God-only trends!"
Some chant self-worth gems,
I sing God-only hymns!
Some say God's Word offends,
I say God's Word amends!
Some are all about them,
Building castles in the sand.
I'm all about Him,
Becoming a God-Man!

More Than You Know - Part 2

Do you want to make an impact for Jesus?

What is your story? Where has the Lord brought you from? What has He done in your life? What kinds of thinking patterns did you have before the Lord? and now after? What has life been like since you decided to follow Jesus?

These are just a few of the questions to ask ourselves when faced with the looming question, "What do I have to offer?"

I have great news for you today!

The answer is: More than you know!

If there is one thing I know for sure about the Lord, it's that He still saves, heals, and delivers to the utmost!

He is not in the business of entering our lives, tossing us lifelines, and then disappearing. He is in it for the long haul!

That is amazing news!

He said He would never leave us, nor forsake us. The Bible says that He becomes the Bishop of our souls, the Author and Finisher of our faith.

So how does this relate to what we have to offer others?

Short answer: EVERYTHING!

When we walk with the Lord, He does a complete overhaul of our lives from the inside out!

Listen, you don't have to have some crazy testimony. For

example, you might not have been strung out on drugs, robbing banks, or stealing cars before Jesus found you. You might not have lived some wretched life of sin for years, burnt all your relationship bridges, or gone through some super-traumatic event that left a huge scar on your life.

But maybe you did…

Whatever the case may be, Jesus is still the same yesterday, today, and forever!

If you know Him, if you have fully surrendered your life to Him, He has done a work in your life, and He is continuing to do so!

He is light!

He is truth!

He repels any darkness and dispels any lie!

So I ask again, what has He done in your life? Well these are the very things you can share with others!

Freely we have received, therefore freely we should give!

No matter your financial status, your job, your living situation, your church home, or your political affiliation. No matter the color of your skin, or your gender…

Pick a thing!

It doesn't matter!

You have more to offer than you know because you know the One who transcends all of those things!

His name is Jesus, and He wants to use you to make an impact in the lives of those around you!

What has he done in your life? What gifts and talents has He given you? Share those things with others!

When you do, you will be amazed at how He will begin to multiply those things in your life!

Perhaps you have been feeling stuck? Like nothing you do truly matters?

Perhaps you have been seeking purpose in your life?

The solution is simple: Start right where you are with what you already have!

It is way more than you know!

I want to encourage you today!

Write down what the Lord has done in your life. Write down some of the things He has blessed you with...

Then begin prayerfully seeking the Lord on how you can share those things with others!

Challenge Corner

- What is your story? Your testimony?

_____

_____

_____

_____

_____

_____

_____

_____

_____

_____

_____

_____

_____

_____

_____

- Where did the Lord find you? How did the Lord find you?

_____

_____

_____

_____

_____

_____

_____

_____

_____

_____

_____

_____

_____

_____

_____

_____

_____

_____

_____

_____

_____

_____

_____

_____

_____

- Never underestimate your story! Remember: it's really God's story anyway! When we share that story for others, we are really bragging on God, and that's always a good thing. He is so good, so wise, and only He can orchestrate things so precisely to bring about the changes in our life that He has! Tell someone about it!

- If you are shy about sharing your faith with others, or sharing your story with others, ask yourself why? Is it because you are ashamed? Scared? Think that your story is too ugly? Not ugly enough? Be encouraged: your story is unique! You alone can impact specific people that no one else can. So don't be scared or intimidated. Go before the Lord and ask Him for the boldness to share your story. Then after that, always remember to attach the gospel to it. For it is the gospel that is the power of God unto salvation in someone's life. It is our story that causes them to let down their guard, open up their hearts, and receive that message!

- You have more to offer than you know! Why? Because of what Jesus has done in and through you. Each of us is a work in progress. But don't let that hinder you from sharing what the Lord has done in you. When we give away what we have freely been given, we make room for the Lord to pour more into us, to expand our hearts! Give and it shall be given!

_____
_____
_____
_____
_____
_____
_____
_____
_____
_____
_____
_____
_____
_____
_____
_____
_____
_____
_____
_____
_____

"And let us not grow weary while doing good, for in due season we shall reap if we do not lose heart." ~Galatians 6:9 (NKJV)

Mornings with Jesus

"SEEK AND YOU SHALL FIND"

Z	T	E	N	I	L	E	F	I	L	O	Z	H	L	M	H	E
Y	L	P	I	T	L	U	M	T	E	S	T	I	M	O	N	Y
X	Q	K	Q	H	Z	S	D	N	E	C	S	N	A	R	T	F
V	L	S	Q	K	L	N	E	L	F	E	L	P	M	I	S	H
J	A	O	M	W	J	Y	L	E	E	R	F	L	C	T	X	F
A	Q	N	O	I	T	U	L	O	S	V	G	R	I	K	T	U
O	X	P	V	M	E	K	A	S	R	O	F	R	E	V	E	N
S	M	F	G	C	I	T	A	M	U	A	R	T	G	O	J	B
L	S	T	O	R	Y	N	P	M	O	C	U	A	V	C	D	M
E	S	U	I	N	F	U	G	I	S	W	J	E	U	E	E	F
P	X	C	J	S	R	C	C	E	K	R	R	Q	Z	J	T	F
E	Z	Q	A	P	D	F	E	T	S	H	L	A	Q	X	V	V
R	E	F	O	R	N	K	C	G	A	I	M	P	A	C	T	K
P	G	S	A	G	I	A	H	U	Z	A	I	X	R	Y	C	J
E	E	L	D	N	Q	J	L	G	V	R	K	Z	O	U	D	Y
E	H	J	G	S	L	E	P	S	I	D	C	E	T	M	P	A
E	N	E	V	E	R	L	E	A	V	E	B	S	J	J	M	E

Dispels	Freely	Traumatic
Story	Looming	Never Leave
Testimony	Solution	Repels
Amazed	Impact	Simple
Multiply	Transcends	Stuck
Overhaul	Purpose	Seek
Scar	Lifeline	Never Forsake

Now unto him that is able to do exceeding abundantly above all that we ask or think, according to the power that worketh in us...
(Ephesians 3:20)

Josiah's Testimony

(Following is a testimony from my youngest son, Josiah, of how God chased him down!)

———————————————

Growing up, I knew who Jesus was.

I served at my church often. Our family was there every Wednesday and every weekend.

When I was 10, I got my first taste of the world. One of my closest friends turned her back on me because she heard something about me that was not true. This hurt really bad. I also had some of the friends I grew up in church with choose a new group of friends, and they did not want to include me. I didn't understand what I had done wrong and why I deserved being treated like that. I grew depressed, angry, and blamed God. I told Him I hated Him, and it was all His fault.

I started down a very dark path. After that, I hated my life and wanted to end it. I wanted to commit suicide, but never had the courage to do it, and then I found pornography!

I tried it once and was instantly hooked. It was the only thing keeping me happy, so I kept doing it.

As the months went by, I got really good at playing different roles for my parents, for my friends, and for people at church.

I was drowning in my sin.

Until one night, when the Holy Spirit spoke to my dad and told him to check on me because he felt something was off.

That night, I got caught. It was one of the most eye-opening experiences of my life. My parents were shocked and heartbroken that I was involved in such a thing because my dad had walked through this very same thing and was very open about the consequences and the pain that came from opening the door to pornography.

My mom was devastated, and she cried openly.

I felt such a wave of guilt, but also relief because, secretly, I had been begging God to free me from this sin.

Looking back, I am so thankful that God loved me enough to chase me down. I confessed to God that I was wrong and begged for forgiveness!

A few days later, I went to a youth retreat and I knew that I never wanted to go back to my old life.

God has been doing such a mighty work in my life, restoring my relationship with Him, with my parents, and teaching me to see who I am in Christ.

Even though I have been freed and forgiven, there still remains a daily struggle, but the more I seek Him and His Word, the more I realize I don't want to go back, and I don't have to!

In Christ,

Josiah Samuel Zeitz

"Therefore if the Son
makes you free,
you shall be free indeed."
~John 8:36 (NJKV)

Start

By: Josiah Samuel Zeitz

Christian-ese
on their knees
what's wrong with these
never have fun
why don't they run?
So strict they got their gun
U mess up they're gonna pull the trigger
getting fat on the word their getting bigger
I was one of them
Never had problems, a perfect gem
God never did anything for me
why should I serve Him?
Sin is funner
Satan took his shot he got me like a hunter
Sin with pleasure? that's a stunner
Christian life? Yeah, I'm done with that
Secrets and lies having fun with that
Taking a bite of the world and I'm getting fat

The demon in the other room
Wears a mask so they don't leave too soon
ask what I want? I already got the moon!
Then I got caught
"it will never happen" is what I thought
Jesus is the one I fought
It's been too long
thought I was right, but I was so so wrong
My heart thrown around like a game of pong
but Jesus saved my life and now my sin is gone!
God is my shepherd and I'm his fawn
I wanna serve Him with all my heart
I messed up but He forgave me so today,
I start...

"But God demonstrates His own love toward us, in that while we were still sinners, Christ died for us." ~Romans 5:8 (NKJV)

The Mundane Mandate

"Even though I walk through the [sunless] *valley of the shadow of death, I fear no evil, for You are with me; Your rod* [to protect] *and Your staff [to guide], they comfort and console me."* ~Psalms 23:4 (AMP)

If you've ever written, then perhaps you have come face to face with something called writer's block.

This involves staring at the paper or the computer screen in front of you and just drawing a blank. You want to write, but nothing is coming to you. The feeling can be quite frustrating and even make you feel hopeless.

However, there are numerous ways past this! I would say the best way is simply, live life! Opportunities have a way of presenting themselves to you around every corner. So rather than focusing on the stumbling block in front of you, get busy living, giving, and praising!

Sometimes in our Christian walk, we have times like these that arise. We may feel useless, unproductive, weary, and to be frank, fed up with life.

Why is this? I think the number one reason is that we have come to realize that this world is not our home. The old ways of doing and thinking no longer satisfy, and for good reason: We have a much higher calling!

Listen, we all face slumps, obstacles, challenges, setbacks, and feelings of inadequacy, but I have great news for you today! The Lord is with you always, walking with you through the valleys and the times when life seems to be mundane.

He is always there to empower you, lead you, and give you purpose and direction!

Sometimes we just need to get away, to spend some one-on-one time with the Lord and ask Him, "Lord, what would you have me do?"

When we build a habit of listening to the Lord, life will no longer feel boring or mundane. And honestly, it's in these moments of valley that we can draw even closer to the Lord— where we can focus in on the things that truly matter!

Life doesn't have to be about "go here, do that, have that, or buy this" to be fun. Rather, when our focus is on Jesus, He refocuses us on people, on eternity, on the things that truly matter!

Have a case of writer's block in your Christian walk? Run to Jesus! He is the answer! Get busy living, giving, and praising. You have a high calling on your life!

"Let us not grow weary
or become discouraged in doing good,
for at the proper time we will reap,
if we do not give in."
~Galatians 6:9 (AMP)

Remaining consistent and faithful will position us to receive God's "And Suddenly!"

Challenge Corner

- Do you ever feel stuck? Inadequate? Useless? Bored? What are some practical ways to get out of these slumps? Hint: When we worship and praise the Lord, He pulls us up to where He is, sets our feet on solid ground, gives us proper perspective - eternal perspective. He puts us on assignment, and suddenly life becomes an adventure, full of "get-to's" and not just "have-to's!"

- The storms of life come to us all. To think that we are always going to have grand mountaintop experiences with the Lord (or that we are supposed to) is entirely false! Our Christian walk will oftentimes be a series of mundane mandates and then BAM! God loves to show up, show out, and do "and suddenlies" in our life! He is the Master at this, catching us doing something right, being faithful, giving, praising, and simply living life for Him and with Him! We need not trudge through life simply scraping by. He wants us to live life to the full, to have abundant life. But that means we will have to go through some valleys. The good news is this however: that He has promised to walk THROUGH the valleys with us!

- Are you discouraged right now? Have you been discouraged at some point in the past? Remember: you are not alone! If you have dealt with this, there is a 100% chance someone else nearby you has as well or is right now! Go ahead, pray about and reach out to someone today! By doing this, you will find purpose beyond your pain, and you could very well change another life for eternity! This is where the adventure lies! This is how to turn seemingly mundane moments into mandates from the Lord!

Mornings with Jesus

"SEEK AND YOU SHALL FIND"

H	I	G	H	E	R	C	A	L	L	I	N	G	R	P	A	N
W	N	S	Y	B	H	C	H	A	L	L	E	N	G	E	S	J
S	E	A	E	N	W	Z	K	F	V	E	Q	F	O	S	G	T
K	V	V	L	F	D	J	U	K	M	S	S	N	W	G	S	S
C	I	U	L	O	Y	D	R	I	P	R	C	R	S	F	P	U
A	T	Y	A	C	Y	U	T	R	K	O	I	E	K	L	M	S
B	C	E	V	U	C	G	A	H	M	T	I	W	E	I	U	E
T	U	A	E	S	N	I	A	F	E	T	C	M	M	S	L	J
E	D	S	M	O	S	H	O	R	I	M	L	A	I	T	S	O
S	O	V	L	I	F	R	S	N	G	K	N	N	T	E	T	T
E	R	E	N	H	T	B	U	I	I	O	V	D	T	N	T	N
N	P	G	L	T	L	T	X	L	V	W	T	A	U	I	N	U
A	N	P	S	O	R	H	I	T	I	I	W	T	O	N	P	R
D	U	S	C	O	S	V	W	N	N	U	G	E	B	G	R	Q
N	U	K	P	T	I	N	M	L	G	S	V	M	A	V	L	F
U	M	P	B	N	V	I	O	J	O	Y	D	L	M	M	A	F
M	O	N	G	E	O	G	N	C	T	I	B	A	H	N	Z	Y

Higher Calling
Comfort
Living
Giving
Praising
Opportunities
Unproductive

Slumps
Mandate
Long Time
About Time
Habit
Listening
Focus

Console
Writers Block
Challenges
Valley
Mundane
Setbacks
Run to Jesus

Blessed is the man that walketh not in the counsel of the ungodly, nor standeth in the way of sinners, nor sitteth in the seat of the scornful.
But his delight is in the law of the Lord; and in his law doth he meditate day and night.
(Psalms 1:1,2)

Think Good Thoughts!

You ever had your thoughts run wild on you?

It can happen in the most peculiar places, like work or church, during a movie, or dare I say while someone is trying to talk with you.

This isn't always a bad thing. But for a Christian, most of our battles are won or lost in the mind. The enemy knows that, and he will use whatever he can to throw his fiery darts our way!

The perfect way to combat these wayward thoughts is by speaking and meditating on the word of God!

Perhaps you've heard it said that you are what you eat? Similarly, we are what we *think* as well! Therefore, it is imperative that we learn to cultivate a good thought life by using the Word of God.

Today's encouragement comes from Philippians 4:8-9 (NKJV).

Paul writes:

"Finally, brethren, whatever things are true, whatever things are noble, whatever things are just, whatever things are pure, whatever things are lovely, whatever things are of good report, if there is any virtue and if there is anything praiseworthy - meditate on these things. The things which you learned and received and heard and saw in me, these do, and the God of peace will be with you."

The more Word we have on the inside, the less room we will have for anything the enemy might throw at us!

Also, the more Word we have on the inside, the more prepared we will be to stand against his wiles!

Today's challenge for us is to meditate on the Word of God!

We can do this simply by finding one or two scriptures and mauling them over in our minds. Speak them out loud. Memorize them! Write them down!

Do this over and again until that scripture just becomes a part of you!

The more we practice this, the better we will become at it, and the more Word we will have in our arsenal!

Think good thoughts!!!

Challenge Corner

- Can you recall an awkward time when a wayward thought (or many thoughts) bombarded you? Don't worry, you are not alone! The thing to remember is this: thoughts come to us all, and it's not a sin or sinful to have thoughts come our way. The sin part happens when we know the thoughts are evil and we continue to pursue them, to think further upon them and eventually act upon them.

_____

_____

_____

_____

_____

_____

_____

_____

_____

_____

_____

_____

_____

_____

_____

- What are some practical ways to combat wayward thoughts? In today's encouragement section, we discussed the importance of meditating on and speaking the Word! It looks something like this: Let's suppose a thought comes our way that has something to do with wanting to do harm to us or our family, what a great chance to speak the word, *"No weapon formed against me shall prosper!"* (See Isaiah 54:17)

_____
_____
_____
_____
_____
_____
_____
_____
_____
_____
_____
_____
_____
_____
_____
_____
_____
_____
_____
_____
_____
_____
_____
_____
_____
_____

- We can't give what we don't have. Therefore, it is imperative that we daily search the scriptures, making it a habit of putting the Word of God in our hearts. Why? Jesus said it perfectly, *"Man does not live by bread alone, but by every word that proceeds from the mouth of God."* (See Matthew 4:4) Listen, the storms of life come to us all and when they do, that is not the time to be scrambling, looking for the right scripture to stand on. If we will be faithful to put the Word in on a consistent basis, (even when the sun is shining) the Holy Spirit will be faithful to draw it out of us at the proper time, when the storms arise!

Is there a poem, rap, or prayer on your heart today?

_____
_____
_____
_____
_____
_____
_____
_____
_____
_____
_____
_____
_____
_____
_____
_____
_____
_____
_____
_____
_____
_____
_____

> If we are faithful to put the Word in, the Holy
> Spirit will be faithful to bring it out!

Mornings with Jesus ☀

"SEEK AND YOU SHALL FIND"

D	G	N	I	T	A	T	I	D	E	M	V	T	G	C	N	W
M	L	B	E	T	X	R	C	V	N	M	P	Q	M	E	W	O
T	R	F	T	U	J	N	H	K	O	E	E	D	D	V	J	B
O	Y	D	N	I	M	J	A	B	B	T	C	U	M	I	N	L
D	U	T	Z	P	Z	N	J	V	L	A	U	C	N	T	U	G
X	L	W	A	Y	W	A	R	D	E	V	L	K	D	A	S	O
N	H	I	D	B	I	E	A	X	A	I	I	J	W	R	T	C
D	M	M	W	O	M	S	K	A	H	T	A	W	F	E	H	D
U	W	W	O	N	D	O	M	H	M	L	R	P	I	P	G	G
C	Y	R	E	I	F	D	C	A	E	U	U	N	M	U	N	
U	Q	D	J	L	W	Y	U	F	D	C	K	F	J	I	O	I
D	A	R	T	S	Q	L	Z	C	W	X	C	T	G	I	H	K
J	N	H	E	E	Z	I	R	O	M	E	M	S	S	T	T	A
S	C	R	I	P	T	U	R	E	I	R	H	S	Y	O	J	E
W	H	A	T	E	V	E	R	Q	Y	U	B	G	R	W	L	P
Z	G	Y	Q	L	Y	B	A	T	T	L	E	S	C	Q	Q	S
G	F	G	B	O	M	D	G	I	Z	Y	L	E	V	O	L	Q

Cultivate	Lost	Wayward
Whatever	Noble	Mind
Fiery	Thoughts	Wild
Lovely	Speaking	Memorize
Combat	Battles	Maul
Won	Scripture	Peculiar
Imperative	Darts	Meditating

The fear of the Lord is the beginning of knowledge: but fools despise wisdom and instruction.
(Proverbs 1:7)

The Broken Places
By: Joshua Scott Zeitz

shore up the broken places
ravaged by sin
the hurts, the pains, the empty spaces
dreams
brought to an end
pillars crumble
towers fall
lopsided lean-to's
where lofty ideals
once stood tall!
poison permeates
death decimates
bitterness chokes and steals
beauty resonates
Light radiates
the Word it stokes and heals!
sparks take flight
embers reignite
Hope
from death to life!
A Father to the fatherless
His Love embraces
His Goodness leads to life
He heals all the broken places!

It Is finished!

Just before Jesus drew His last breath, after suffering the most excruciating torture, after a crown of thorns was placed upon His head, after the nails were driven into His hands and His feet, after they spat upon Him, and slapped Him, and beat Him beyond recognition, after they ripped the beard from His face, after they hurled insults and mockeries at Him, He hung there on that old rugged cross, the very symbol of the curse that was placed upon mankind.

He became the curse.

He bore our sin, our sickness, and our shame!

He hung on that cross, gasping for air. He looked up to Heaven and cried, "Father forgive them, for they know not what they do!" The very weight of all eternity was upon His shoulders. He hung on that cross, rejected by both man and God. The enemy laughed, and all Hell rejoiced… But He wasn't done yet! With one final breath, The King of kings and Lord of lords, bolstered His last bit of strength and declared boldly and triumphantly, IT IS FINISHED!!!

It is finished!!!

The price for sin was paid in full.

With His dying breath, the Prince of Glory's blood satisfied the wrath of a Holy, Righteous, and Just God!

It is finished!!

What does that mean for you and me in everyday life?

It means that no matter what comes against you today, no matter what anyone says about you, no matter what the enemy hurls your

191

way or the world tries to place on you, no matter what fear or anxious thought tries to steal your joy, it is finished!!

If God be for you, who can be against you?

My challenge for you and I today is to declare boldly that it is finished!

When you are tempted to fret or worry or fall prey to comparison Christianity (which really isn't Christ-like at all), when that devil comes a-knocking on your door today, don't open that door.
Instead, declare triumphantly, "It is finished!"

You have this today because He *has this*. He defeated, de-toothed, and de-clawed the enemy!

IT IS FINISHED!!

Challenge Corner

- Sometimes we need to just remind ourselves of what Jesus has done for us, in us, and through us. Sometimes we need to take a step back, or maybe a few steps back and just worship Him for who He is - not asking anything from Him, just basking in His presence, in His goodness! When we do that, our miniscule problems will melt away.

_____

_____

_____

_____

_____

_____

_____

_____

_____

_____

_____

_____

- What do you have to be thankful for today? What has Jesus done in your life? Tell Him today how much He means to you! If you aren't where you want to be in your relationship with Him today, don't fret. Run to Him! He longs to spend time with you. He loves you with an everlasting love!

Is there a poem, rap, or prayer on your heart today?

Mornings with Jesus ☼

"SEEK AND YOU SHALL FIND"

B	O	D	I	K	U	C	B	R	E	J	E	C	T	E	D	V
P	L	Z	F	I	F	N	R	L	O	B	M	Y	S	Y	L	S
Z	W	S	F	K	D	Q	A	O	A	K	W	T	D	D	G	L
W	V	O	Z	Q	I	W	M	I	S	S	S	R	E	J	F	X
T	Q	Y	S	H	A	M	E	M	L	S	G	I	T	P	Y	G
J	X	M	Y	R	P	S	B	X	Q	S	D	U	O	Y	R	N
D	X	D	E	T	A	E	F	E	D	S	E	M	O	N	O	I
E	R	O	B	R	V	D	K	T	P	I	H	P	T	K	L	L
B	E	A	R	D	F	E	R	I	L	C	S	H	H	R	G	R
S	Z	T	Q	R	U	C	M	U	S	K	I	A	E	U	F	U
N	D	H	G	T	I	L	Z	X	E	N	N	N	D	G	O	H
V	Y	O	T	G	N	A	P	V	V	E	I	T	O	G	E	B
J	W	R	I	B	A	W	X	A	L	S	F	L	T	E	C	Y
A	B	N	G	L	W	E	F	P	U	S	H	Y	X	D	N	M
K	V	S	L	O	H	D	H	T	A	E	R	B	Y	C	I	X
C	E	B	O	L	D	L	Y	U	D	S	C	Y	K	L	R	C
Y	A	D	Y	R	E	V	E	I	S	X	F	Y	D	U	P	R

Declared	Detoothed	Cross
Triumphantly	Thorns	Hurling
Rejected	Boldly	Prince of Glory
Beard	Everyday	Symbol
Nails	Breath	Shame
Rugged	Defeated	Paid
Finished	Sickness	Bore

But thou, O Lord, art a shield for me; my glory, and the lifter up of mine head.
(Psalms 3:3)

Pull Back the Curtain

"But the fruit of the Spirit is love, joy, peace, longsuffering, kindness, goodness, faithfulness, gentleness, self-control. Against such there is no law."
~Galatians 5:22-23 (NKJV)

One of my favorite things about a hotel room is the heavy curtains that frequently hang in front of the windows. They allow you to sleep in longer, blocking the light from spilling in.

It's easy to lose track of time with such heavy curtains, however. You open your eyes, and it's very dark in the room. You think to yourself, "It can't be later than 4 or 5 in the morning." Then someone goes and pulls back the curtains, causing instant blindness to everyone inside! You look at the clock on the table, and it reads 9:30. What?!!!

You ever catch yourself praying for more patience? More faith? Peace? You ever say something like this: "Oh God! Give me patience to deal with so and so?"

If so, you're not alone.

But I have good news for you! Pull back the curtains: you already have all the patience, peace, faith, goodness, and self-control you will ever need. You might not feel it. It might not look like it. But you have all of these characteristics! They are probably just hidden behind some heavy curtains.

Listen, the Word of God is described as a lamp unto our feet and a light onto our path. (See Psalm 119:105) The more Word we allow in our lives, the more light we allow into our lives, and in turn, the more of Him we allow in our lives!

When we pull back the curtains and allow the Word to spill into our rooms (our hearts), impatience has to flee! Unforgiveness has to go! Anger has to subside!

It's really a simple matter of replacing old ways of thinking and doing, with the Word!

If you are a born-again believer, the Spirit of God dwells inside of you! You have the fruit of the Spirit! Claim it, speak it. Draw them out by pulling back the curtains and allowing the Word to get into every nook and cranny of your life.

This I say then, walk in the Spirit, and you won't gratify the desires of the flesh. (See Galatians 5:16)

Pull back the curtains and allow the Word to wash over you today, cleaning you, refining you, and renewing you!

Challenge Corner

- You ever catch yourself praying for more patience? Joy? Peace? Praying for things that God has already equipped you with is easy to do when you're focused on the issues at hand. But if (or when) we choose to pull back the curtains of God's Word, we will begin to see from His perspective and realize that we already have what we are praying for. We just need to receive His gifts and walk in them.

- What are some practical ways we can pull back the curtains of God's Word in our lives on a more consistent basis? (Suggestions: build a habit of learning a new scripture each week, or write down scriptures and place them around your home where you will see them often!)

_____
_____
_____
_____
_____
_____
_____
_____
_____
_____
_____
_____
_____
_____
_____
_____
_____
_____
_____
_____
_____
_____
_____
_____
_____
_____
_____

Mornings with Jesus

"SEEK AND YOU SHALL FIND"

O	K	U	T	R	W	E	N	W	S	T	I	U	R	F	C	Z
N	L	R	R	E	F	I	N	I	N	G	S	O	F	R	E	T
V	G	J	B	H	R	T	T	S	R	E	G	N	A	E	V	H
S	R	N	P	G	V	K	L	H	E	C	N	E	I	T	A	P
S	E	J	I	F	S	L	B	E	B	I	T	T	N	R	K	U
J	N	G	X	L	E	M	O	W	Z	Q	W	Q	B	P	V	K
T	E	O	M	W	L	X	P	C	N	I	A	T	R	U	C	C
O	W	X	D	S	R	I	R	N	U	B	L	Z	C	M	R	A
D	I	I	T	N	P	A	P	X	O	F	B	L	T	A	X	B
A	N	L	S	T	N	E	H	S	O	O	O	I	C	M	S	L
Y	G	O	Q	N	S	M	A	I	M	C	K	W	V	D	S	L
Q	Z	T	Y	Z	U	H	V	C	K	X	A	W	N	G	E	U
D	Y	K	H	A	B	V	V	L	E	R	A	F	F	V	N	P
P	E	S	J	R	S	P	X	I	I	A	L	J	V	X	D	R
U	A	P	B	A	I	B	Q	G	Q	E	U	T	K	A	N	B
W	Z	N	D	Q	D	Q	N	H	E	V	V	Q	H	B	I	V
J	H	H	O	T	E	L	S	T	X	O	A	N	S	I	K	L

Kindness	Cranny	Fret
Flee	Clock	Wash
Patience	Renewing	Hotel
Refining	Fruit	Pull Back
Nook	Dwells	Today
Anger	Curtain	Light
Subside	Peace	Spilling

This is the day which the Lord hath made; we will rejoice and be glad in it. (Psalms 118:24)

199

Stay the Course

"Let thine eyes look right on
and let thine eyelids look straight before thee.
Ponder the path of thy feet
and let all thy ways be established.
Turn not to the right hand
nor to the left:
remove thy foot from evil."
~Proverbs 4:25-27 (KJV)

Have you ever been to a giant amusement park, museum, or zoo? Some of these places can be huge and difficult to navigate, especially if you want to see everything.

Personally, I tend to find enjoyment in the simple things and can spend quite a lot of time in one spot, especially the aquarium. I can sit and watch the fish swim for a long time!

Granted, it may seem like you aren't getting your money's worth if you don't see every single thing, but sometimes less is more. And there *is* such a thing as quality over quantity.

In our Christian walk, it can be difficult at times to stay focused. There are so many distractions out there, sometimes within our very own homes.

Listen, the enemy wants nothing more than to steal, kill, and destroy all the time. And Jesus wants nothing more than to bring us life, and it more abundantly all the time!

However, this doesn't mean life is going to be an amusement park all the time. Sometimes it's in the quiet moments, the moments which may appear to be mundane or pointless at first that we are challenged the most!

It's in these times of stillness that it can be easy to lose focus, get distracted, fall back into old ways of thinking and doing, and basically forfeit progress.

Can I encourage you? Don't give up!

Learn to accept these moments of mundaneness as moments to draw closer to the Lord, to grow in character. Character and integrity are often built the most when no one is watching—except you and the Lord. Allowing Him to mold and make us in the secret place is what prepares us for the public space.

Preparation time is not wasted time!

Be encouraged today, just because you aren't seeing things happening right now perhaps, just because you don't feel things changing, or just because you may think the Lord doesn't see, hear or care, He does!

He always does and He always will!

Draw close to Him today! He doesn't use lots of bells and whistles to get our attention. Most often it's just a still, small voice. But it's when we listen to that voice that our relationship with Him will grow the most, and it's in these times when we are being molded into His likeness!

Learn to love the simple things in life and you won't need all the other things to make you happy.

Jesus is more than enough!

Don't Give Up! Stay the Course!

Challenge Corner

- What distractions in your life give you the most trouble? That causes you to go off course if you focus on them too much? Not all distractions are evil or bad; they simply block us from doing the things that we need to get done. For example, watching television is not of the devil, but if we watch television for 48 hours straight and fail to spend time with our family, go to work, or serve others, then the very thing that was meant to bring some temporary happiness or relief has become a hurdle to get over.

- What are some practical steps we can take today to avoid the many distractions that try to keep us from being all we can be, from serving others, or perhaps even from spending time with the Lord?

_____

_____

_____

_____

_____

_____

_____

_____

_____

_____

_____

_____

_____

_____

_____

_____

_____

_____

_____

_____

_____

_____

_____

_____

_____

_____

_____

_____

_____

_____

_____

_____

_____

- Spending time with the Lord or reading the Bible isn't always going to be an awe-inspiring event, but it's still important that we do these things. What are some practical steps we can take to make a habit of getting into the Word and getting away with the Lord every day? Remember: start small and grow tall. These things don't have to happen overnight, but if we are diligent, over time our lives will flourish and our relationship with the Lord will as well!

Mornings with Jesus

"SEEK AND YOU SHALL FIND"

R	X	D	T	R	G	D	C	W	T	R	A	R	Y	P	T	E
Y	H	J	O	E	Q	Z	O	E	B	O	M	L	P	O	N	T
L	G	F	I	L	Y	T	U	J	O	U	G	J	P	N	E	A
J	U	O	P	A	T	J	R	Z	L	U	V	Q	A	D	M	G
K	O	C	D	T	I	Y	S	C	V	M	S	D	H	E	E	I
Z	N	U	I	I	R	E	E	P	J	U	O	G	E	R	S	V
Q	E	S	S	O	G	B	C	E	D	F	P	M	J	K	U	A
E	R	U	T	N	E	V	D	A	R	J	P	J	E	A	M	N
I	L	I	R	S	T	Y	C	Y	T	V	I	U	Q	N	A	D
M	R	T	A	H	N	I	I	H	P	U	Z	U	E	Z	T	A
M	F	T	C	I	I	N	G	V	A	O	A	H	P	F	H	S
U	A	S	T	P	G	S	F	I	O	R	V	O	V	Q	K	L
N	Q	I	I	B	K	V	V	X	I	Q	A	N	K	R	X	G
D	U	M	O	T	P	M	J	U	P	D	O	C	A	X	B	C
A	I	P	N	Q	E	P	M	B	U	W	T	P	T	L	K	N
N	E	L	P	R	E	P	A	R	A	T	I	O	N	E	U	T
E	T	E	D	T	Y	P	K	Y	M	U	E	S	U	M	R	P

Park	Simple	Navigate
Amusement	Zoo	Ponder
Course	Integrity	Quiet
Distraction	Relationship	Adventure
Character	Happy	Aquarium
Preparation	Mundane	Moments
Enough	Focus	Museum

"Delight thyself also in
the LORD; And he shall
give thee the desires
of thine heart."
(Psalm 37:4)

Hope Beyond the Scope!

It is inevitable. Whenever I talk about the goodness of the Lord or His love, someone always messages me and asks, "What about the wrath of God?"

Listen, I get it!

We look out into the world, we turn on the news, or we go to work even, and it is clear that people need Jesus! And many of us want nothing more than to have God step in and take care of the mess we see all around us.

But today I want to give you some encouragement!

I want to provide you with hope beyond the scope!

Have you ever heard the expression "failing to see the forest for the trees?"

Simply put, this means that it is often difficult to see the bigger picture (in this scenario, the forest), because we get so hung up on the smaller things around us, right in front of us (the trees, if you will).

There is no doubt that this world has gone crazy.

But this world has been crazy for a long time. And Jesus, who is the same yesterday, today, and forever, has been here all the while, providing peace, power, grace, and hope to whosoever will receive it!

We don't have to allow the world and its troubles to bog us down!

We don't have to be swayed by this or that virus that arises!

We don't have to be shaken by this or that bad news report!

Do we hide in the sand? No.

Do we hide in our churches? No.

Then what's the answer!

We need to seek Jesus daily, allowing Him to be our source.

If all we do is focus on the wrath of God, the judgment of God on those around us, we will miss the many opportunities to be *like* God to those around us!

There is coming a time when all things will be made right, when all things will be made even and just. But until that day comes, I want to encourage you to work out your own salvation with fear and trembling.

Go before the Lord every day, seeking Him with your whole heart and asking Him to create in you a clean heart, to make you a vessel He can use to reach the world around you!

When we do that, He will bring us up where He is. He will give us proper perspective and an eternal mindset, and we won't be consumed with the cares of this life. And we will have hope beyond the scope—a hope we can freely share with others!

> Never allow what others say or think about you to stop you from sharing the hope you have through Jesus!

Never Let You Down

By: Joshua Scott Zeitz

Are you lost or lonely?
Feeling Overwhelmed?
Let the Bible be your compass!
Let Jesus take the helm!

Are you sinking in the deep?
Feel like you're gonna drown?
Cry out to Jesus!
He'll never let you down!

Mornings with Jesus

"SEEK AND YOU SHALL FIND"

U	F	W	P	S	Z	K	C	N	M	I	Y	G	W	T	R	E	M	B	L	I	N	G	L	O
G	S	U	E	H	V	P	G	V	O	U	P	E	R	S	P	E	C	T	I	V	E	X	C	Q
D	S	M	J	E	Z	N	O	T	I	K	T	Q	E	F	S	E	E	R	T	J	F	Z	Z	S
B	A	D	D	W	I	C	S	R	C	H	Z	N	P	B	A	X	C	I	M	J	U	V	O	C
X	X	G	V	W	Y	U	D	Y	Y	P	C	P	W	W	T	X	Z	M	H	P	V	C	G	X
A	Y	H	O	J	J	W	O	X	W	O	V	E	L	E	S	S	E	V	D	D	Y	R	D	F
X	A	L	E	N	D	I	J	E	U	A	E	E	E	E	J	A	C	F	A	I	F	A	W	Z
Y	L	L	C	P	B	C	E	R	C	T	K	T	T	U	U	T	O	H	L	H	C	Z	O	Q
A	X	C	F	S	K	N	A	X	W	R	T	Z	C	U	T	G	F	Z	O	C	Y	Y	C	F
G	P	P	L	L	J	G	J	P	P	L	U	U	T	T	T	C	Q	G	C	V	G	K	O	F
N	G	Z	K	R	E	Y	B	S	O	R	O	O	P	S	J	R	J	A	I	B	H	C	R	T
I	A	Y	K	M	Z	G	A	I	P	C	E	Z	S	D	D	E	I	S	T	O	U	Z	P	F
U	N	H	E	V	B	L	W	C	K	K	E	S	I	F	U	A	E	M	S	S	B	F	P	V
A	E	N	I	I	V	Z	O	K	L	J	Q	P	S	M	I	T	L	C	X	W	G	B	E	X
N	T	X	V	A	Y	K	W	U	U	J	Z	W	Q	I	O	E	Y	D	P	A	A	M	F	I
G	Q	K	T	S	T	U	W	R	C	S	Z	T	S	H	O	G	A	A	S	I	D	Y	I	J
X	E	I	T	B	M	N	A	H	A	L	B	N	F	W	B	N	K	A	S	Y	G	D	E	E
B	O	E	S	V	A	R	R	D	O	T	E	P	Q	N	G	V	L	R	C	H	D	M	O	D
N	X	E	T	S	E	T	X	N	Q	S	H	A	N	E	W	S	W	F	H	B	L	E	Y	H
F	F	J	T	K	V	X	J	O	N	H	O	J	N	K	J	I	T	P	L	S	F	A	I	L
N	B	C	E	A	V	K	J	Y	M	V	S	E	Q	H	M	K	X	C	T	T	D	C	G	K
E	X	P	K	N	G	O	M	E	S	Q	C	S	V	Z	E	Y	Z	T	R	I	Q	K	Z	N
A	O	B	M	S	X	Z	K	B	R	V	O	S	O	E	D	A	T	X	G	Q	Q	P	T	H
H	X	Q	V	C	R	O	L	D	L	L	P	C	T	D	R	S	R	K	D	L	R	P	H	D
V	W	Y	E	V	E	B	N	A	R	A	E	Q	R	Q	J	G	K	T	A	J	N	H	G	K

Hope	Source	Crazy
Beyond	Vessel	Create
Scope	Perspective	Trembling
Swayed	Focus	Salvation
Allowing	Whosoever	Clean Heart
Wrath	Expression	Trees
Encouragement	News	Just

It is of the Lord's mercies that we are not consumed, because his compassions fail not. They are new every morning: great is thy faithfulness. (Lamentations 3:22,23)

Final Notes:

Scripture Index:

Be sure to check out Joshua's Podcast, available on all major outlets (Spotify, Apple, etc.):

Mornings With Jesus

Ways To Connect with Joshua Scott Zeitz:

Email: captivatedhope@gmail.com

Web: https://jszbooks.com/

YouTube Channel:
https://www.youtube.com/@joshuazeitz2029

You won't want to miss Joshua's interview on **CBN**:
https://www.youtube.com/watch?v=UewZ5emH7XI

Books by Joshua Scott Zeitz:

Rags to Riches   February 2018
~A Story of God's Unfailing Love

Ripe for Harvest   August 2021
~Winning Your World for Jesus

Mornings with Jesus
~ A 30 Day Journey Devotional Series:

Mornings with Jesus ~ Ask   May 2022
~**Ask** and it Shall be Given

Mornings with Jesus ~ Seek   March 2023
~**Seek** and You Shall Find

Mornings with Jesus ~ Knock   Coming Soon
~**Knock** and the Door Will be Opened

"What we make happen for others,
God will make happen for us!"

~Joshua Scott Zeitz, Podcast Motto

Made in the USA
Columbia, SC
12 December 2023

28337194R00126